Berg Women's Series

Simone de Beauvoir

A Critical View

Renee Winegarten

BERG *Oxford / New York / Hamburg*

Distributed exclusively in the US and Canada by
St. Martin's Press, New York

Published in 1988 by
Berg Publishers Limited
Market House, Deddington, Oxford, OX5 4SW
175 Fifth Avenue/Room 400, New York, NY 10010, USA
Schenefelder Landstr. 14K, 2000 Hamburg 55, FRG

British Library Cataloguing in Publication Data

Winegarten, Renee
  Simone de Beauvoir: a critical view.
  1. Beauvoir, Simone de—Biography
  2. Authors, French—20th century—
  Biography
  I. Title
  843'.912   PQ2603.E362Z/

ISBN 0–85496–151–8

Library of Congress Cataloging-in-Publication Data

Winegarten, Renee.
  Simone de Beauvoir.

  Bibliography: p.
  Includes index.
  1. Beauvoir, Simone de, 1908–   —Criticism
and interpretation.   I. Title.
PQ2603.E362294   1987   848'.91409   87–23858
ISBN 0–85496–151–8

Printed in Great Britain by Billings and Sons, Worcester

Contents

To Asher — in ever-loving memory

Acknowledgements

Translations from French works are my own, except those taken from *America Day by Day* and *The Long March*.

Grateful thanks are due to the following publishers, notably to Gallimard, for quotations from the works of Simone de Beauvoir and Jean-Paul Sartre; and to Nagel (her *L'Existentialisme et la sagesse des nations*); Seuil (F. Jeanson, *Simone de Beauvoir ou l'entreprise de vivre*); Perrin (C. Francis & F. Gontier, *Simone de Beauvoir*); Julliard (Raymond Aron, *Mémoires*); Grasset (Olivier Todd, *Un Fils rebelle*); University Press of New England (Richard Cobb, *French and Germans, Germans and French*); Heinemann (Herbert R. Lottman, *The Left Bank*); Weidenfeld and Nicolson (*Living with Koestler: Mamaine Koestler's Letters*, ed. C. Goodman); Hutchinson (A.C. Koestler, *Stranger on the Square*); Duckworth (*America Day by Day*); Deutsch/Weidenfeld (*The Long March*); Signet (Mary McCarthy, *The Humanist in the Bathtub*); Cedric Chivers (Nelson Algren, *The Man with the Golden Arm*); Arbor House (Nelson Algren, *The Devil's Stocking*); Morrow (Madsen, *Hearts and Minds*); Collins/Harvill (Solzhenitsyn, *The Oak and the Calf*); Chatto and Windus/Hogarth Press (A. Schwarzer, *Simone de Beauvoir To-day*); Gollancz (Betty Friedan, *It Changed My Life*).

1 The 'Great Affair'

Simone de Beauvoir — novelist, autobiographer, moral and political essayist, permanent rebel and Leftist, fellow-traveller, witness of contemporary affairs and events, student of social problems, indefatigable protester against injustice, pioneer of modern feminism — stands as one of the most influential and controversial writers of the twentieth century. 'Writing has remained the great affair of my life', she declared when past sixty in 1972.[1]

It is curious, and surely noteworthy, that she did not apply these words, 'the great affair of my life', to her long relationship with the existentialist philosopher, novelist and dramatist, Jean-Paul Sartre, vital as that liaison was to her, indeed to them both. There seems no reason to doubt the validity of that statement of hers. One of the most important facts about her is that she saw herself primarily as a writer and an intellectual at a period when the value of literature itself was seriously under question; and when French intellectuals still occupied, or sometimes liked to think that they occupied, a position of immense significance and influence not only in France but in the world at large. Writers no longer tend to speak publicly with such confidence and faith in the act of writing itself, whatever their private views or wishes might be; while the role that Jean-Paul Sartre and Simone de Beauvoir sought to play on the world political scene in the years after 1945 has not so far been emulated.

That she was a writer and an intellectual were titles she claimed with pride and not a little satisfaction. These titles were not lightly won: she worked extremely hard all her life, first at her studies and then at her writing. 'A day in which I don't write leaves a taste of ashes', she owned to an interviewer in later years.[2] In the first flush of enthusiasm that she felt at engaging upon a new work (so she relates), she thought nothing of writing as much as three or four hundred pages at a stretch, and this as part of a first draft to be cast aside. Neither she nor Sartre were models of conciseness. She could spend six or seven hours a day at her desk. Diaries, letters, essays or articles were penned as well

1

as her novels and her social studies of contemporary attitudes and prejudices.

It was a very considerable outpouring, though nothing like as vast in scope and as innovative as that of George Sand. Once, Simone de Beauvoir remarked that her reason for living was writing, not action (and not personal relationships). Much as she liked to stress her love of nature, her delight in the manifold aspects of life — good food, travel, friendship, and above all the greatly emphasised 'success' of her relationship with Sartre — nevertheless there is a sense in which her work came first. Everything served as fuel for composition — and that included Sartre himself who looms large transformed in various guises in her fiction or as leading actor in her memoirs.

Writing was for her an adventure: she found in it a kind of exaltation. Moreover, for one who was always deeply conscious of the transience of human affairs, it was a way of leaving a record, of conquering time, of bequeathing to her fellow-creatures some trace of her brief passage on the earth. It could be a form of liberation, too, enabling her to escape from her constricting milieu, and eventually providing her with a career and livelihood, and thus with independence. She saw writing also as a means of trying to tell the truth about herself, of seeking to understand herself and her world, and as a way of communicating this truth and this understanding to others. That, at least, was the avowed aim. How far she succeeded in conveying the truth must remain a matter for debate. There were subjects on which she preferred to stay discreet. It was only in later years that she alluded to some of these omissions, without expatiating upon them. If she did not exactly wish to perpetuate some flattering image of herself, none the less one of her aims was 'to be loved' through her writings.[3] How to be loved without pleasing?

Indeed, with every condemnation of her youthful self-deception, or through her later criticism of her own works, she presents herself as the seeker after truth, the plain-speaking, plain-dealing, no nonsense advocate of 'authenticity': that is, she develops the image of a personality endowed with admirable qualities. 'Authenticity' figures, after all, as the highest existentialist virtue, and in Sartre's opinion she possessed it in greater degree than himself. Even Jean-Jacques Rousseau, confessing his youthful misdeeds, or Jean-Paul Sartre, sardonically looking back on the misconceptions of his childhood self, place themselves at the vantage-point of their mature attitude at the moment of writing. It would seem that autobiographers, whatever their ostensible intentions, cannot avoid this trap of being wise after the event, and even of appearing attractive through giving the impression of telling all in complete honesty. Only on reflection does the reader come to realise the limits of authorial honesty, the motives for it, or the price paid for it by others (relatives, friends, lovers) who figure in the tale.

The main problem for the young Simone de Beauvoir who wanted to be a writer from an early age — and who made many false starts before she published her novel, *L'Invitée*, in 1943 — was the question of what to write about. In accordance with traditional advice, she mostly chose to stay close to herself and her own experience: indeed, whenever she tried to depart from this decision her work was inclined to be bloodless. Basically, she was not an inventive or highly imaginative writer. Her originality lay rather in the rigour with which she pursued certain existential insights.

Her major works are deeply personal: the novels, *L'Invitée* and *Les Mandarins*, for instance, where she elaborates upon actual situations and crises in which she has found herself; or the influential *Le Deuxième Sexe*, which studies the condition and fate of womankind past and present, and which may be regarded partly as a form of generalisation drawn from her own experience and conceptions. Then there is the whole collection of substantial autobiographical volumes: *Mémoires d'une jeune fille rangée*, *La Force de l'âge*, *La Force des choses*, *Tout compte fait*; and including the searing account of her mother's death from cancer, *Une Mort très douce*; and her book on Sartre's decline into blindness and senility, *La Cérémonie des adieux*. This multi-volume autobiography, composed between 1956 and 1981, remains her monument, as well as an essential document for understanding her era.

In itself the personal life of a writer and intellectual who spends a good deal of the day engaged in discussion and in writing would seem unlikely to offer much matter of passionate excitement, unless the author happens to be deeply introspective and attuned to the adventures of the inner self or spirit. The Sartrian version of existentialist philosophy, to which Simone de Beauvoir adhered and which she herself expounded, rejected the very notion of 'the

3

spiritual'. This philosophy was not only materialist in outlook but also opposed to the Freudian conception of the unconscious. It is therefore less in introspection than in the nature of her keen response to the process of living, to the life of the mind, to the major trends and crises of the day that Simone de Beauvoir's memoirs still foster enquiry and debate.

To compose an autobiography that will interest a large number of readers, as indeed with the composition of any literary work, the author has to control and give narrative and dramatic shape to a mass of formless material. Simone de Beauvoir who — like Sartre — always sought a wide readership, was no exception. We have to rely on her for the account she gives of her childhood and adolescence. Although this account is based on her diaries, on letters and the recollections of close friends, it is her own attitude to her origins, background and youthful self that proves significant. We have to rely upon her, too, for the interpretation she gives of her early years — and it is worth remembering that she wrote the first volume of her autobiography, *Mémoires d'une jeune fille rangée*, when she was forty-eight to fifty. Her conception of life was by then firm and fixed within the borders of existentialist philosophy as defined by Jean-Paul Sartre, and of his political evolution.

How far is autobiography self-invention? What reliance should be placed on memory, which is known to be treacherous? What role is played in composition by the present idea that the writer has of a past self? It would be mistaken to imagine that Simone de Beauvoir was unaware of these questions. She said once: 'I shouldn't like to forego this exciting impression that literature still occasionally gives me: through creating a book, to create myself in the dimension of the imaginary'.[4] When she wrote those words she was nearing the end of her undertaking as an autobiographer.

Clearly, as the work progressed, she felt dissatisfied with the more or less straightforward chronological narrative form she had adopted for the first three volumes of her autobiography. She tried to justify her choice of chronological order as a way of portraying the passage of time, her changing relationship to it and to a changed world. She complained about the very nature of autobiography, above all about its apparent inability to convey the large part played by her writing, its character and its importance to her. This very dissatisfaction led her to abandon chronology in *Tout compte fait* for the discussion of separate themes which she felt to be important in her life. Such a treatment actually proves much more repetitive and less attractive than the chronological method employed in the earlier volumes.

Ever present there loomed Sartre's short autobiographical masterpiece, *Les Mots*, that savage and witty dissection and indictment of a childhood misspent in literature conceived as the cultural prerogative of an elite. Although Sartre's book was not published until 1963, it was in large part written in 1954, that is, some two years before Simone de Beauvoir undertook the first volume of her own autobiography. If she did not adopt Sartre's rigorous and highly original method, which was perfectly well known to her, it was because her intentions were different from his. She was not primarily concerned with the analysis of what Sartre called a literary 'neurosis', but with trying to account for the substance of her own existence and development, recording the conflicting attitudes of her tempestuous era, and examining the progressive variations in the ideas and actions of Sartre as well as her own. (Sartre never attempted to do the same for her: it seems that the first time he spoke publicly and at length about his relationship with Simone de Beauvoir was in an interview as late as 1965.) Given her intention to record, she was naturally drawn to a more traditional form of autobiography.

Once Simone de Beauvoir observed: 'I am a writer', defining herself as a serious 'woman writer'.[5] That remark is only superficially self-evident. At first, she appeared to be completely absorbed in the established masculine view of the world. Nothing reveals this more clearly than the vocabulary of her early philosophical and literary studies. There, she adopts without demur — like so many nineteenth-century women writers — a masculine persona, in her general use of 'man', 'the young man', 'mankind', and 'men', when discussing her own ideas and opinions. It was only gradually that she perceived how her own outlook was a privileged one, how she was in some sort a pioneer, and how her sensibility and experience were not completely identical with those of her male colleagues. This discovery was to prove of great importance for her later development, and also for the awakening of many of her feminine readers. In this sense, the realisation that she was not only a writer but also 'a woman writer' was thus not something commonplace or obvious but a kind of revelation or conquest.

The course of Simone de Beauvoir's life and her views on it, together with her literary output, will be seen here principally through the prism of her primary activity as 'a writer and a woman writer'. Both terms are needed because of her contribution to the whole question of woman's role in the twentieth century, despite the fact that she had no desire to end in what she characterised as 'a female ghetto'. She herself believed that every position one adopted had to be challenged, though she did not appear to realise that there were certain areas in her thinking, and especially in her political thinking, where she rarely or never did so. To challenge her work by stressing the element of artistic self-creation that is involved in every literary enterprise is simply to pursue a method that she — at least ideally — advocated herself.

One will find in the present undertaking neither the surrogate mother-figure, cherished by those individuals in quest of feminine identity, nor the idol of the utopian revolutionary Left. Moreover, Simone de Beauvoir's relationship with Sartre is not viewed here as one of the great love stories of all time — as her joint biographers, Claude Francis and Fernande Gontier, have oddly ventured to depict it. This study offers rather an attempt to probe the mystifications of an all-too-common modern form of rationalism which leads its adherents to see only what they wish to see, where change and revolution are at stake — whether in personal or public relations. It seeks to examine some of the pitfalls involved in the pursuit of total freedom. And it endeavours to assess the value of Simone de Beauvoir's activity and writings in the spheres of feminism, politics and literature.

Notes

1. *Tout compte fait*, Gallimard, 1972, p. 131.
2. Interview with Caroline Moorehead (2), *The Times*, 16 May 1974.
3. *La Force des choses*, Gallimard, 1963, pp. 368, 677.
4. *Tout compte fait*, p. 152.
5. *La Force des choses*, p. 677.

2 The Rebel

The principal theme of the first volume of Simone de Beauvoir's autobiography, *Mémoires d'une jeune fille rangée*, is the drama of her revolt against her family and class, against their traditional prejudices and values, and the social conventions to which they remained subservient. She tells the story of her gradual liberation from what she perceives as the blinkered and oppressive attitudes not just of her intimate family but of an entire class; and in telling it, she reveals how she found her subject and how she became a writer. It is from the forward position of her liberated self that she sees the nature of her early enslavement to received ideas and her courageous rebellion against them. This sometimes leads to the awkward situation where the child or the adolescent is portrayed as having thoughts and opinions beyond her years. The question of her exact age is often left vague in the discussion of the development of her outlook. There is, moreover, an implied political message as well as a social and literary point to the work's intentions, and this political thread dates from the moment of writing, not from the period that is being described.

By the time she came to write the narrative of her upbringing, she had naturally been influenced by social and political circumstance, by friends, and by her reading which included the writings of Marx. It was Marx and Engels who maintained (in their early work, *Die Deutsche Ideologie*) that the ideas of the ruling class are in every epoch the ruling ideas; and that the class which is the ruling material force of society is at the same time its ruling intellectual force. This highly questionable notion, which would be absorbed by Jean-Paul Sartre, makes no allowance for the powerful influence of dissent, criticism and satire, especially in French literature since the eighteenth century at least. Nor does it take into account the world-wide radiance of French writers and thinkers, from Voltaire onwards, as a subversive force. The very place of Sartre and Simone de Beauvoir themselves — who, at their peak, enjoyed the veritable veneration of intellectual circles, from Europe to Africa and Latin America and beyond, in their role as tireless and sometimes immoderate critics of authority and society — challenges the Marxian view of the dominant powers of the intellect being at one with an entire ruling class. It is none the less an idea that has gained widespread currency: the members of the bourgeoisie are seen not only as the ruling force but as the instigators or perpetrators of a predominant high-sounding ideology, constructed purely for their own self-interest.

According to Simone de Beauvoir in 'Faut-il brûler Sade?' (a partial apologia for that detestable libertine), the 'divine Marquis' passionately denounced 'the bourgeois mystification which lies in giving one's class interests the force of universal principles'. And she added: '. . . what Sade notably understood is that the ideology of his time merely gives expression to an economic system and that, by materially transforming this system, the mystifications of bourgeois morality will be annihilated'.[1] Any complex whole of specifically bourgeois ideas, if it existed, would not be as monolithic as Simone de Beauvoir implies. Some distinction should be made between, say, liberal and ultra-Rightist, instead of lumping together — as she does in her essay on contemporary right-wing thought — everyone who is not on the Left or the extreme Left, and regarding such so-called middle-class writers as proponents of a single evil bourgeois doctrine. The worst aspect of this Marxian standpoint is that people are no longer judged as individuals with a share of virtues and shortcomings, but solely as the representatives of an evil, exploitative class or mass. In effect, it resembles the bias of judging people to be harmful because of their race or religion, a view which Simone de Beauvoir otherwise abhorred. On the subject of the bourgeois class, however, she could see no redeeming feature whatsoever, and this prejudice colours her entire work.

What precisely was the character of the obstacle that stood in her way, and to what extent were her strictures justified?

Less than forty years before Simone de Beauvoir was born in Paris in 1908 there had occurred what was, up to then, the worst and most humiliating defeat in French history: the Prussian victory over the armies of the Emperor Napoléon III at Sedan in 1870, and the collapse of the Second Empire. German soldiers who were besieging Paris looked down from the heights upon

Frenchmen in the act of killing Frenchmen when the Paris Commune fell to the Versaillais (the forces of the French government resident at Versailles). The Commune passed into legend and controversy, an object of veneration to the Left and of loathing to the Right. Simone de Beauvoir's paternal grandfather, for instance, was still holding forth about the hated Communards years after their demise. The wall against which the last defenders of the Commune were shot, known as *le mur des Fédérés*, remains a place of pilgrimage for demonstrators against injustice down to the present day. This bloody struggle to the death was one more episode in the virtual civil war that had raged at intervals in France since the Revolution of 1789, and especially since the Terror of 1793–4, whose victims were actually outnumbered by those who were slaughtered in the last days of the Commune.

The miasma left by the defeat of 1870, and by the social conflicts exacerbated by the Commune and the manner of its end, naturally haunted the generation of Simone de Beauvoir's parents. They lived through a period of soul-searching and of increasing nationalism, presented in seductive guise by an anarchist dandy who became a committed nationalist, the Lorraine-born Maurice Barrès. The desire for revenge, for the recovery of the provinces of Alsace and Lorraine, lost to the Germans, was nurtured up to the French victory in the Great War of 1914–18, when they were finally recovered. The Third Republic, born of defeat on 4 September 1870, and widely unloved, was to survive up to the Fall of France in 1940. From the beginning it was marked by conspiracies engineered by royalists or Bonapartists, by dissension between Catholics and secularists, and by acrimonious and sometimes violent clashes between adherents of Left and Right.

The most extraordinary and severe moral test of the Third Republic lasted twelve years, from 1894 to 1906. This was the notorious Dreyfus Affair. A well-to-do and unpopular Jewish army officer, Captain Alfred Dreyfus, wrongly accused of treason and condemned to the penal colony of Devil's Island, was not rehabilitated until 1906, after a tormented struggle. Was the fate of one miserable man, and a Jew to boot, to weigh against the reputation of the French Army (a particularly sensitive subject just then) or the ultimate destiny of the French nation? Those who took a moral stand on the rights of the individual believed

9

that it should. Others equally passionately did not.

The Affair divided brother against brother, friend against friend. The hugely influential right-wing movement known as Action Française was founded during the Affair. (The first issue of its newspaper appeared in the year of Simone de Beauvoir's birth.) Royalist, pro-Catholic, often from French nationalist sentiment rather than religion, and proto-fascist, it would profoundly affect the ambience of an entire era, and in particular the character and tone of the Vichy regime of 1940–4. Its founder, Charles Maurras, that powerful stylist but virulent polemicist, was to cry out at his trial and conviction in 1945: 'It is Dreyfus's revenge!' Such was the lasting resonance of the Affair.

It was in the course of the battle to preserve or undo the injustice suffered by Dreyfus that the noun 'intellectual', the appellation which Simone de Beauvoir would so loudly claim, entered common French usage. The word was employed to define those writers, university teachers, scholars and thinkers, who felt passionately enough about what was happening and about the principles involved to speak out in public. Outstanding among these was the author of *Germinal*, Emile Zola, tried and convicted for his open letter, 'J'accuse', in support of Dreyfus. Zola, founder of the Ligue des droits de l'homme, followed the path taken earlier by Voltaire and by Victor Hugo. He helped, with them, to establish firmly in the public mind the idea of the writer and thinker as a fighter for a righteous cause. Whether, in the future, the chosen cause would be as just or as clear-cut as that of establishing the innocence of Dreyfus, could prove a highly subjective matter in the years to come, when the manipulative arts of skilfully concealed propaganda and counter-propaganda were to become current.

The influence of Maurice Barrès and of Charles Maurras throughout the first half of the twentieth century — different from each other as they were, though united in their detestation of Dreyfus and his supporters — can scarcely be overestimated. Their writings affected opponents as well as adherents, because their stand could not be ignored. The atmosphere of intense nationalist feeling that they fostered inevitably coloured the outlook of Simone de Beauvoir's father — and hers too, through her early imitation of it and her later reactions against it.

Her parents were both offspring of the right-thinking bourgeoisie. Her father, Georges de Beauvoir, a younger son proud of having a handle to his name, however obscure, came from a family of functionaries and regarded himself as being on the fringes of the aristocracy. Françoise de Beauvoir, née Brasseur, her mother, was born into a wealthy provincial banking family. She remained a devout and practising Catholic, devoted to good works, until the days of her last illness; and she saw to it that her two daughters, Simone and Hélène, were educated at Catholic schools. The matter of their salvation was of deep concern to her. In contrast, her husband was a sceptic, indifferent or hostile where religion was at stake. The difference between Simone's parents on this theme, common enough between married partners in that age, was to lead her later to question not just the Catholic religion but everything that received the orthodox imprimatur of authority.

Three people in particular stand out in her indictment of the role of the bourgeoisie in her early life: her father, her mother, and Mme L. . . (known as 'Mme Mabille' in her autobiography), the mother of her best friend, Zaza.

Simone de Beauvoir is not at all generous to her father. As a small child, she adored him. This was the time when she queened it over her younger sister, Hélène, and ordered her about. It was the period of utter security that she was afterwards to perceive as a kind of false paradise, but 'lost paradise' none the less. In her 'Pour une Morale de l'ambiguïté' (1947), the child is seen as living in ignorance in a world already made and fixed by others. Eventually, the time of questioning arrives: 'Why *must* one behave in this way? What purpose does it serve? And if I behaved differently, what would happen?'[2] With adolescence, and the realisation of the contradictions and weaknesses of adults who were earlier unquestioningly obeyed and admired, the world begins to lose its settled appearance. And with adolescence comes the painful moment of individual choice and freedom. The grown person will always preserve 'the nostalgia' for the time when, as a child, he remained unaware of the demands of freedom, declared Simone de Beauvoir. This seemingly objective and theoretical account of the child and adolescent in general was to be confirmed by the account given in *Mémoires d'une jeune fille rangée*, and it offers, in brief, a summary of her own progress in existentialist terms — a progress that requires an obstacle, an opponent, a villain to be challenged, for its drama: the role fulfilled by the bourgeoisie in the person of her parents and others encountered in the course of her early education.

At first it may seem odd that, writing in the 1950s, though reflecting on her childhood and adolescence which occurred before, during and after the First World War, Simone de Beauvoir should still be obsessed with the damaging values of a class that had been ridiculed, despised, and exposed to brilliant effect by so many of the great French poets, novelists, artists, thinkers, from the early years of the nineteenth century onwards. These creative figures, from Stendhal and Daumier to Baudelaire and Flaubert and beyond, though often themselves born into the middle class, had reserved their satire or their venom for the bourgeoisie, accusing it of complacency, concern with materialist values, blinkered stupidity, indifference to the fate of the less privileged in society, among other crimes.

This kind of estrangement from one's family origins and background was therefore nothing new. It was registered by André Gide, a novelist she admired in her youth, with his disdain for received morality in the celebrated cry: 'Families! I hate you!' It was shared by the Surrealists, who functioned as the leading literary and artistic movement of the interwar years, with their anarchic outrages aimed to shock and provoke the bourgeoisie. Simone de Beauvoir would later allude to this kind of bourgeois hostility to the bourgeoisie, to be found among eminent predecessors, but she considered this variety to be distinct from her own which (like Sartre's) sought the actual liquidation of an entire class.

What was the reason for this continuing bitter hostility? That there was an oppressive stuffiness in French middle-class life, and notably in the bourgeois provincial circles from which Simone de Beauvoir's mother issued, can scarcely be denied. Things were still 'done' or 'not done'. Family gatherings, however tedious, had to be attended with docility; opinions and usages that might have served fifty or sixty years before were still current. Marriages, for instance, continued to be 'arranged'. The bridegroom was granted a large measure of liberty in his style of life; his bride was expected to be a convent-educated virgin who brought with her a sizeable dowry, and who was ordained to preserve the family virtue. It was customary for the groom to be considerably older than his bride, as was the case with Simone de Beauvoir's parents: her father being thirty, her mother twenty-one at the time of Simone's birth. The great virtue was conformity: submission to the prevailing social conventions, conventions which had survived in 'decent society' for longer than anyone could remember and which — above all — must be *seen* to be obeyed. Hence the ground for the accusation of hypocrisy that was so often levelled at the middle class.

These customs had not changed much, if at all, by the time Simone de Beauvoir was growing up. Her role in life, given her background, was fixed: ideally she should make a good marriage and raise a family. This destiny of the 'well-brought-up girl' was shattered by the 1914–18 War which reduced her father's financial status from that of the bourgeoisie to that of the 'new poor'. Already, many of his hopes for money and social position had been dashed by the liquidation of his father-in-law's bank, followed by that gentleman's imprisonment. Georges de Beauvoir was not paid the dowry that was promised him; nor would he ever be able to provide a dowry for either of his daughters. Henceforward, he and his family were *déclassés*. Perhaps that, too, was one source of her resentment against the class which no longer considered her to be quite acceptable.

Georges de Beauvoir had not seriously pursued the legal profession for which he was trained, having preferred to lead the life of a man-about-town to be found at the races and at bridge parties, or taking part with his wife in amateur theatricals. Financial difficulties brought this agreeable life to an end: only his womanising and his drinking continued. Embittered by his fate, he engaged in acrimonious quarrels with his wife over money. Simone de Beauvoir would allude bitterly to his infidelities, to those 'knife slashes into the marriage contract' which he felt were permitted to men.[3] The double standard of sexual morality, denounced long before by Mme de Staël and George Sand, was still flourishing.

A good conversationalist and a charmer, with his love of the theatre and his love of books, at first Georges de Beauvoir encouraged his young daughter's reading. He was gratified by her intellectual success, yet he disliked 'bluestockings'. It seemed to her that after a time he transferred his affections to her sister

13

Hélène and (as she was to tell Francis Jeanson) she felt betrayed.[4] This sense of betrayal goes some way to explain her lasting hostility to her father. Even his cultivated mind is not spared, for she sees his culture as a kind of escape, and as the prerogative of an educated elite. Like the rest of his class, she maintains, he believed that anything to do with culture was reserved for the bourgeoisie. The possession of culture made the bourgeois feel superior to everybody else. Her father was polite only to the well-born, she relates, but he threw his weight about with inferiors.

On her father's political opinions, Simone de Beauvoir remains equally and tellingly relentless. While he did not envisage the restoration of the monarchy, he admired Charles Maurras and, moreover, without actually being affiliated to Action Française, he had friends among the Camelots du Roi, its often upper-crust bully-boys. Nationalism was not a matter to be questioned: he called it his 'sole religion'. He loathed 'métèques' ('dagos', 'wogs'), and 'was as convinced of the guilt of Dreyfus as my mother was of the existence of God'.[5] The idea that French Jews should participate in the nation's affairs made him furious. That his daughter chose to be a teacher could not really please him: in his opinion, teachers belonged with the dangerous sect of intellectuals who had supported Dreyfus and who had sacrificed their native land, their race, class and family in the name of the vicious nonsense that was ruining France and civilisation as a whole: that is to say, 'the Rights of Man', pacifism, internationalism, socialism. He was afraid lest his daughter, through her profession, should come to adopt such dreadful views.

That she did so, and was writing her autobiography from a 'socialist' standpoint, shows less that a teaching career led to their adoption, than that her outlook was to become the direct opposite of her father's on every matter. The anti-nationalist stand she was to take in opposition to the French government during the Algerian War in the 1950s and early 1960s, for instance, would have horrified her father, had he lived to see it. Her final comment on his death in July 1941 is still icy with rancour: 'My father was precisely at one with his social image: his class and he himself spoke through his mouth with one voice. His last words: "You earned your living early on, whereas your sister cost me dear", were not an encouragement to tears'.[6] For Simone de Beauvoir, in her polemic, 'La Pensée de droite, aujourd'hui'

(1955), published not long before the first volume of her autobiography, right-wing thought is identical with bourgeois thought, the expression of a hated class.

If she remained unceasing in her opposition to the bourgeoisie, it was doubtless because she heard in it her father's voice. Worse still, she remembered how his opinions had coloured hers in her early years. Once, for instance, her father had read to her from Gobineau's influential *Essai sur l'inégalité des races humaines*, and she had then adopted its racial theories. She had also followed her father unthinkingly in finding it amusing when the Camelots du Roi forced people they disliked to drink castor oil. When she began to reflect on things for herself, therefore, it was he with whom she would be locked in permanent battle. And this is perhaps one reason why the fight against the bourgeoisie continued, even long after she had to all appearances freed herself from its clutches and its prejudices. She could never really be liberated from her enduring hatred of the bourgeoisie because she could not erase either such memories or her origins, and this stain (as she felt it to be) simply fostered ever more loathing of a class that in her childhood and girlhood had marked her for its own.

Her attitude to her mother was eventually to become rather more understanding, particularly in her account of her mother's death, *Une Mort très douce*. But their relationship was not an easy one. Georges de Beauvoir's infidelities turned his wife into a domineering, possessive mother. Simone had to study and work where her mother could keep an eye on her, so doors had to be left ajar. Françoise de Beauvoir refused to allow her daughters to swim or to ride bicycles. She opened their letters. She could not bear to feel excluded from their amusements, and wanted to join them when they met their friends. The very close attachment between her two girls aroused her jealousy. None the less, there were occasions when she could be supportive. In the end, Simone de Beauvoir saw her mother as a woman who had been largely mutilated by her repressive upbringing and damaged by an unsatisfactory marriage. There were bitter battles between them during the years of adolescent revolt, yet 'if she poisoned several years of my life, I paid her back in full without doing so deliberately', Simone de Beauvoir reflected afterwards.[7] She could not resist comparing the manner of her mother's death, however, with that of the aged poor who die alone and neglected, remarking that

15

her mother had been cherished and well-cared-for as a 'privileged' person. Though strictly true, the very observation strikes chill.

It was the influence of Françoise de Beauvoir which dominated the girl's early religious education. Simone entered a private Catholic school, the Cours Désir, at the age of five and remained there for twelve years until she was seventeen (when she divided her time between the Institut Catholique and the Institut Sainte-Marie de Neuilly). The early years were spent in pious practices, and with an increasing yearning for perfection and for some mystical experience. She was around twelve when, shutting herself in the lavatory, she tried out various forms of mortification, including rubbing herself hard with pumice stone until she bled, or whipping herself with a gold necklace. Her confessor, unimpressed with her lofty self-accusation about her spiritual shortcomings, rebuked her for more mundane acts of disobedience. So disillusioned was she with his lack of elevation that she sought out another spiritual director elsewhere. The move sowed some disquiet; but her faith in God stayed firm for a while.

A recently discovered notebook that she kept during a retreat, and dated 3–7 April 1922, when she was fourteen, reveals the intensity of her spiritual exercises, her desire to do good to others, her constant condemnation of her own lukewarm responses and backsliding. Already can be heard the note of the fear of death which would pursue her throughout her life: 'Do not let us count on making amends at the last; every minute one must be ready to die. Knowing that one will die is to be forced to live rightly . . . . We must think of these things even if such thoughts crush us'. There can be found, too, a hint of the conflict that would soon undermine the whole spiritual edifice: 'Why hope to attain one's salvation and enjoy life at the same time?' Already there is the dread of wasting any moment, the arrangement of a timetable for meditation, prayer, manual and intellectual tasks: 'Do not engage in fruitless reading or conversation, do not waste time', she advised herself in her notebook.[8]

Then one summer evening when she was about fourteen, a strange thing happened while she was on holiday at Meyrignac, her paternal grandfather's country home in Limousin. It forms a dramatic climax in her autobiography. Leaning on the windowsill, 'I thrust my hand into the cool branches of the cherry-laurel,

I listened to the drip-drip of the water, and I realised that nothing would make me give up earthly delights. "I don't believe in God any more", I said to myself, not particularly surprised'.[9] The delusions of idealism and spirituality, and their damaging consequences, would be given to feminine characters in her early novel with its ironic title, *Quand prime le spirituel* (*When Things of the Spirit Come First*); while other women in her books would experience a similar revelation of loss of faith which is never restored.

She does not seem to have reproached her mother for responsibility in inculcating what she herself saw as spiritual delusions, but rather an entire class for fostering them. Whatever the extent of her later protestations of atheism, though, she was marked by Catholicism for life, not only by *timor mortis* but by the high standards of strict soul-searching, by the desire for and satisfaction in rectitude, by the quest for absolute perfection, and by a deep awareness of the vanity of all human endeavour. The void left by loss of religious faith would have to be filled. Some kind of absolute would have to be found elsewhere to compensate for this loss: at first it would be sought in literature; then later it would function in terms of political certainties.

Despite Françoise de Beauvoir's influential part in her daughter's religious education, she does not appear to play the role of major villainess in a spiritual drama: that role is attributed to the mother of Simone de Beauvoir's friend, Elisabeth, known as Zaza. This lady is portrayed as an 'accomplished specimen of the right-thinking bourgeoisie':[10] mother of nine children, well-to-do and conscious of her social position, a woman for whom social obligations were of prime importance. There was much talk about God and charity in her household, but what really counted were status and money, we are told. The conflict between Action Française and the Church which led to the papal condemnation of the Maurrasian movement in 1926 was a theme of passionate concern in this circle.

For Zaza's mother, young Simone de Beauvoir was a dangerous and disruptive influence as an intellectual and a *déclassée*. Was not the girl preparing to have a career and to teach in a *lycée*, that is, a non-Catholic school? As Simone de Beauvoir tells the story in *Mémoires d'une jeune fille rangée*, Zaza, gifted, intelligent, full of life, is virtually destroyed by the mother she loves, a woman who utterly fails to comprehend her daughter's legitimate aspirations. Torn between a desire for an independent life and an attachment to her mother which leads her to comply with that lady's social demands, the tormented Zaza cannot break free to attain self-realisation. Like Simone, Zaza too felt the urge to be a writer and had long contemplated working on a novel.

All the same, the account of Zaza's decline and death, moving as it is, remains equivocal. It was a drama to which Simone de Beauvoir had tried to give expression in fiction in her earliest attempts at the genre, but without success. She was haunted by it, and returned to the theme later. Perhaps her very uncertainty about the cause of Zaza's death made the whole subject linger and stir her creative imagination. The question remains on reading the autobiography: is Zaza's death due to her frustrated passion for 'Jean Pradelle' (the name given to the future philosopher, Maurice Merleau-Ponty, in *Mémoires d'une jeune fille rangée*)? Does she lose her senses, worn out with sorrow at the (seemingly feeble) excuses he gave for postponing their marriage, because of a high-minded filial obligation to his mother? Is her illness the result of her own mother's demands and objections to the match, although the suitor apparently came of good family and was a practising Catholic? Zaza's feverish condition makes both mothers consent to the marriage, but too late. Or is it that Zaza died tragically of meningitis or encephalitis? — possibilities that the author does envisage. Was it by chance or by choice? — a query that obsessed Simone de Beauvoir as a writer.

The true facts about Zaza's last days were not revealed to her until many years later by the girl's sister, after she had read the account in *Mémoires d'une jeune fille rangée*. Simone de Beauvoir never published the real story (given by Francis and Gontier in their biography of the author),[11] although she could have done so in later volumes of her memoirs. On making the customary pre-nuptial enquiries, Zaza's parents had uncovered a scandal: Maurice Merleau-Ponty's mother had had an affair with a married man, and Maurice and his sister were the natural issue of her lover although they bore her husband's name. The young man learned for the first time from Zaza's father, who had arranged a meeting in the Bois de Boulogne, that his mother had been unfaithful and that he was illegitimate. He promised to give up

Zaza, despite his love for her, and invented unconvincing excuses in his letters to her. That her parents, who tried to encourage a different match, had revealed everything to Zaza, was completely unknown to him. The girl fell into a deep depression, and then into a delirium that culminated in her death.

The major impression left by the account of Zaza's fate in the autobiography, however, is that it serves as an example of maternal domination, bourgeois family repression, masculine obtuseness and insensitivity, denial of an individual's self-fulfilment, suppression of an intelligence and a talent, and unbearable waste. Zaza's destiny, it is made perfectly clear, is what Simone de Beauvoir's could have been, if she had not defied the social conventions and had not persisted in her determination to be a writer against all odds. The intended moral lesson is obvious; the story itself, as told in the autobiography, appears more fluid than this, more strange, even inexplicable. The last words of *Mémoires d'une jeune fille rangée* concerning Zaza's destiny, strike a note that suggests Simone de Beauvoir's indebtedness to her Catholic education: 'Together we had struggled against the degraded fate that lay in wait for us and I long thought that she had paid for my freedom with her death'.[12] Nothing reveals more plainly the enduring effect of spiritual bookkeeping and of her Catholic upbringing on Simone de Beauvoir's sensibility than that final phrase: the notion that one's own life can be redeemed by the sacrifice of another's.

The life and death of Zaza present the negative image of Simone de Beauvoir's conception of her own destiny. It is not just the snuffing out of an intelligence, but the life-denying consequence of sexual repression that is portrayed in the feverish and deranged Zaza when she bursts in upon Mme Merleau-Ponty. Like Zaza, the young Simone envisaged being married and having children. She dreamed of marrying her cousin and childhood companion, Jacques Champigneulles (his surname is given as Laiguillon in her autobiography). His father had died young, his mother had remarried and she left her son to his own devices. He was good-looking, worldly, yet unsure of himself, being inwardly divided between the idea of a comfortable bourgeois existence and the attractions of a bohemian life style. Extremely fond of literature, he, too, talked of writing a novel. He read modern poetry to his young cousin, showed her how to appreciate the paintings of Picasso and Braque, or discussed new avant-garde films and the latest theatrical productions.

To her, he seemed so very sophisticated. He took her into the bars of Montparnasse, then the favoured haunt of artists and writers. Later, she went to local bars on her own, and courted adventure. She soon realised that her nature was different from his. Unstable, frivolous, he liked to take the easy road, whereas she always wanted 'difficulties to conquer'.[13] At nineteen, she was torn between her wish to marry Jacques and her dread of losing her freedom.

Their attachment flickered and revived, only to waver again. Cousin Jacques seemed disinclined to commit himself. She discovered that he was following the pattern of his peers: he had a lower-class mistress whom he would doubtless discard when he settled down. By this time, Simone de Beauvoir had already entered another orbit: she had new interests, and had made new friends at university. She realised (so she relates) that she would never marry Jacques. It was with no little astonishment, however, that she learned he was about to wed a young woman who brought with her a considerable dowry. This marriage would prove a disaster. In his excessive haste for conventional bourgeois success, Jacques ended in financial ruin: he took to women and drink, and died at forty-six. For Simone de Beauvoir, here was another case of promise unfulfilled, of a destructive bourgeois ethos at work.

The account of her relationship with Jacques — was it ever more than youthful friendship, with perhaps the vague possibility of marriage? — stands, like the story of Zaza, as the portrayal of a girl's narrow escape from a dreadful fate. Just as she had eluded being stifled in bourgeois convention by exercising her own strength of will, so she had somehow eluded the misery of a bourgeois marriage. This union between two persons who were largely incompatible, she implies, would have been founded on the sort of romantic dreams and illusions that lead so many girls into an impasse. Caught there, they cannot develop their potentialities to the full.

How Simone de Beauvoir moved from the dream of marrying Jacques to her later expressed conviction that the principle of marriage is 'obscene', seems far from clear. Was she disillusioned with marriage by the 'desertion' of her cousin Jacques? Did the example of her parents' uneasy relationship convince her that bourgeois marriage was a deception? Certainly, some members of the liberated university circle in which she came to move encouraged the rejection of the traditional role for women. Sartre, for instance, made it clear to her that he did not think much of marriage. Her desire for independence and for a professional and literary career did not look compatible with the ties, the compromises, the duties and burdens of matrimony as understood by the middle class of her day.

Like a number of women writers of note before her, including George Eliot (whom she particularly admired) she would choose the path of the free liaison as a token of her liberation. Nor should the role of literature be underestimated. If, as a child, she identified with the tomboy 'intellectual' Jo in Louisa M. Alcott's *Little Women* (though definitely not with the later Jo of *Good Wives*, who declines into matrimony), she felt even closer to Maggie Tulliver who upset the conventions in George Eliot's *The Mill on the Floss*. Other books, bestsellers of the 1920s, were favourites of the budding author. One of these was Margaret Kennedy's romance, *The Constant Nymph*, with its fond depiction of musical bohemia and of Tessa, a spontaneous free spirit. Another was Michael Arlen's once shocking *The Green Hat*, where the heroine takes numerous lovers while remaining devoted to the great love of her life. Novels of this kind encapsulated the 'new morality' of the modern, liberated feminine spirit, characterised by inner integrity, in the years after the end of the First World War.

To write appeared as a means of escape to freedom, the way in which a woman could make a place for herself through her talent. Already, at fifteen, she wanted 'to be a famous author'.[14] This seemed an ambition particularly accessible to women, since so many had found fame through their writings. Books became a passion: 'Literature took the place formerly held by religion in my life, invading it entirely and transfiguring it'.[15] Salvation would come through literature. It was a view she shared then with the young Jean-Paul Sartre. Her meeting with him would be the encounter of two people dominated by literary ambition and by the irrepressible urge to write. Nothing whatsoever would be allowed to interfere with that.

Notes

1. 'Faut-il brûler Sade?', in *Privilèges*, Gallimard, 1955, pp. 69, 71.
2. *Pour une Morale de l'ambiguïté* (1947), Collection Idées, Gallimard, 1983, p. 56.
3. *Mémoires d'une jeune fille rangée*, Gallimard, 1958, p. 189.
4. Francis Jeanson, 'Entretiens avec Simone de Beauvoir', in idem, *Simone de Beauvoir ou l'enterprise de vivre*, Seuil, 1966, pp. 253–4.
5. *Mémoires d'une jeune fille rangée*, p. 38.
6. *Une Mort très douce*, Gallimard, 1964, p. 161.
7. Ibid., p. 160.
8. Jean-Pierre Barou, 'Un Carnet retrouvé: Simone de Beauvoir élève du cours Désir', *Le Monde*, 30 May 1986.
9. *Mémoires d'une jeune fille rangée*, pp. 137–8.
10. Ibid., p. 116.
11. Claude Francis and Fernande Gontier, *Simone de Beauvoir*, Perrin, 1985, pp. 99–100.
12. *Mémoires d'une jeune fille rangée*, p. 359.
13. Ibid., p. 216.
14. Ibid., p. 142.
15. Ibid., p. 186.

3 The 'Special' Relationship

The free union of Simone de Beauvoir and Jean-Paul Sartre, copied, admired, envied, discussed, probed, disputed, stands as the most celebrated and controversial cultural partnership of the age. That she did not regard it as a model to be followed by others did not prevent some from trying to imitate it. This union is central to any discussion of her life and work, though it occupies a less dominating place with Sartre. The nature of their free union which she liked to project as one different from any other of apparently similar variety, would at times prove to be a source of strength to them both, and at times a cause of pain and distress (largely to her; at any rate, he did not choose to discuss publicly its ups and downs in an autobiography). Over the years — and their liaison endured half a century from 1929 until Sartre's death in 1980 — it changed in character from a sexual union to a close intellectual friendship which she qualified in later life as a form of 'osmosis'.

One problem about their relationship arises principally from the fact that it is her viewpoint which predominates (although where their fiction is concerned they both alluded obliquely to the state of the affair at different times). Sartre's letters to her and to other women, letters which she published after his death, and which are selected and edited by her, do shed some light on it, indirectly as well as directly. Her own replies, however, have to be deduced from his tone or his allusions to her fears and anxieties, and his repeated efforts to reassure her, since she did not make her side of the correspondence public.

The ideal condition of such a union is expressed by Pierre, the figure loosely modelled on Sartre in her novel, *L' Invitée*: 'One of us cannot be defined without the other'.[1] Sartre himself, despite his frequent protestations of eternal devotion in his letters to her, did not say quite as much. He told her at various times he fancied that they were two consciousnesses melted together; that their mutual relations were 'idyllic'; that 'you are me'; that no couple could be more united than they were; that the whole world, including his mother, would take second place to her.[2] But he did not set out to show that he could not be defined without her, however closely their fates might be intertwined. In his eyes, surely, and in those of his readers and his audience, his work could stand alone. Perhaps that is one reason why his autobiography, *Les Mots*, ends well before his first meeting with her.

It is she who, through her chronological account of the development of Sartre's thought and responses in her autobiography, has made herself indispensable for any study of his life and writings. It seems to have been vitally important to her that her unique place in Sartre's career should be recognised, and any potential encroachment upon it would be seen as a threat. In her last years, if anyone attempted to suggest that the 'special' relationship was not so special after all, or to hint that their union was not built on perfect trust and complete truthfulness — although she permitted herself to acknowledge certain notable strains in it — that rash person would arouse her ire. One who ventured so far could expect to be slapped down publicly. Where Sartre bounds free, she can scarcely be defined without him, and that is largely her own doing.

Simone de Beauvoir first met Sartre in 1929 when she was twenty-one. He was two and a half years older. She was studying for her degree at the Sorbonne, and at the same time she was preparing for the *agrégation* (in philosophy) at the Ecole Normale Supérieure, the qualification required for teachers in state schools or *lycées*. Among her contemporaries were Simone Weil, who would become known as a single-minded religious thinker and political activist, and Claude Lévi-Strauss, the future social anthropologist. It was at this period that she was attracted to a fellow student, René Maheu (whom she calls 'André Herbaud' in her memoirs), a friend of Sartre's.

René Maheu was married, and their mutual attraction has been qualified by Simone de Beauvoir as an *amitié amoureuse*, essentially platonic. He it was who gave her the nickname that she retained throughout her life, *le Castor* or the Beaver ('Beaver' being treated as an English transliteration of Beauvoir). From afar, she observed the exclusive band around Sartre and his friend, Paul Nizan, a group that had already acquired some notoriety at the Ecole Normale Supérieure. For his part, Sartre had noticed her, endowed as she was with striking, dark good looks; and, through Maheu, he sent her a drawing of 'Leibniz bathing with the Monads'. Sartre had learned that she was studying Leibniz as her special subject under Léon Brunschvicg, who was then (according to Sartre's fellow student, Raymond Aron), 'the leading Mandarin' at the Sorbonne.[3] With Nizan, Sartre invited her to study with them in preparation for the oral examination of the *agrégation*: 'From now on, I am taking you in charge', said Sartre.[4]

In 1929, then, the possibility of marriage with her cousin Jacques faded from view; and the association with Maheu came to an end when he failed his examination and withdrew to his provincial home, leaving Sartre in command of the field. As a joke, many years later, Simone de Beauvoir was to say that she was attracted to Sartre because as a student he was 'the dirtiest and the ugliest' of her contemporaries.[5] He felt very self-conscious about his appearance, owing to his small stature and his wall-eye, but people usually agreed that he was transfigured once he began to talk.

Certainly, he remained immensely attractive to the opposite sex, and he made it perfectly clear from the start that he did not expect to be confining his attentions to one woman alone for the rest of his life. Speaking to Sartre in 1974, Simone de Beauvoir recalled how '. . . you told me straightaway, when we got to know each other, that you were polygamous, that you had no intention of limiting yourself to one woman only, that was understood; you have indeed had affairs . . .' .[6] What did this frank expression of Sartre's polygamous intent or Don Juan-ism mean to a young woman who had been as 'well brought-up' as Simone de Beauvoir, and who had proved so passionately intense in her friendship with Zaza? On his lips, no doubt, it all sounded different, modern, adventurous, revolutionary even, when stated so candidly. Yet to act the Don Juan, and without particular reproof, had long been a man's privilege — indeed, one enjoyed by her father, much to her own distaste. The fact that this partnership of theirs was to reject the bonds of bourgeois marriage must have made it sound particularly daring. She might be, at twenty-one, the youngest *agrégée de philosophie* in the whole of France, second only to Sartre, but she would never forget that he had come first in the examination. He retained a certain aura of intellectual superiority in her eyes. It made her especially receptive to his ideas.

Clearly, their 'arrangement', which suited Sartre so well, carried with it the specious attraction of total freedom, the foundation of his early thought. She herself was anxious to be rid of the whole 'right-thinking' bias of her family, and what could be more likely to upset her parents than a plunge into 'free love' and a bohemian style of life? Sartre and Simone de Beauvoir would never set up house in a joint establishment of their own: they occupied rooms in different but nearby hotels; or sometimes they lived on separate floors in the same hotel (and later, in separate apartments). This absence of a shared home she regarded as one aspect of the central originality of their relationship. They did not want to be burdened with domestic responsibilities. They did not want children, seen as part of the oppressive bourgeois family set-up. According to Paul Nizan's widow (who knew them both at university), in their early days they lived in bohemian disorder in their hotel rooms amid unwashed plates, completely unconcerned by the mess. It was a classical situation for middle-class rebels of the period.

In Sartre's phraseology, theirs was a 'necessary love', while his affairs with other women would be 'contingent loves' and hence of a secondary nature. Their understanding would be permanent, any other unions would be temporary. Perhaps that did not sound so bad, from her point of view, for hers was to be the primary, dominant and secure position. The theory was that relationships with others would permit them both to experience a gamut of feelings, sensations, pleasures, that could only prove enriching to them as human beings and as writers. The autobiography leaves the impression that both of them were of this opinion, rather than that the view was his alone (and this is confirmed by a remark he made later on).

According to Simone de Beauvoir in the second volume of her autobiography, *La Force de l'âge*, it was Sartre who suggested that they formulate an 'arrangement' to last two years. 'I complied', she wrote, as if there were no discussion on her part, stressing her sense of security: ' . . . I knew that no misfortune would ever come to me through him, unless he were to die before I did'.[7] During the period of the 'arrangement', they were not supposed to make use of the freedom that they had theoretically granted to

26

each other. The important thing was to avoid a decline into constraint and habit. In a significant further 'pact', they agreed that they would never lie to each other. There was to be total candour and complete sincerity between them.

In short, they were expecting to create and live in a virtually utopian situation, of the sort that they would aim for in their political pronouncements. What they wanted was to remake human relations in a new and superior form, apparently unaware of the sheer hubris implied by this intention. For human relations may well be improved, through greater awareness and concern for the sensibilities and the well-being of other people, but it seems unlikely that human limitations can be totally overcome, even by exceptional beings. Their own experience was to bear this out only too well.

It would be Simone de Beauvoir's belief (after Sartre) that 'most of the members of the bourgeoisie' cannot have a real relationship with the truth. Unlike other 'petit-bourgeois intellectuals', the two of them had (he said) *a real understanding of the truth*, that is certainly something: but that did not in any way imply that we have *a true understanding of reality*'.[8] To have such a 'true understanding of reality' they would have had to be born to suffering in the proletariat. However, complete frankness in their own relationship was clearly something that they felt set them apart. Whatever their professed detestation of 'elitism' in any form, their sense of superiority to the rest of the middle-class intellectuals of their day is here made manifest, no matter how far their own position falls short of the utopian ideal.

They are superior because they are aware of the ineradicable 'disability' they suffer on account of their privileged place in society, whereas most of the members of their class are said to lack such an awareness. They are superior, too, it is suggested, because they have promised to tell each other all, whereas other 'petit-bourgeois intellectuals' necessarily flounder in lies and self-deception. Their fiction, in depicting largely the negative aspects of their ideal aspirations, conveys a different and possibly even a truer idea of their actual relationship in some of its modes. And the reader may well wonder why they both chose to stress such negative aspects in their novels.

As regards the commitment to total candour, it is clear that this was a delusion. Sartre, it is true, in his letters to her, made no secret of the intimate details of his numerous affairs with other women; sometimes, as with the student called 'Martine Bourdin', revealing a strain of caddishness that could not but upset his 'special' partner and earn her reproof. At times, in the tone of his letters to her, he recalls the Marquis de Valmont in Choderlos de Laclos's novel, *Les Liaisons dangereuses*, through his sexual confidences making Simone de Beauvoir as it were an accomplice.

The author of *La Force de l'âge* once remarked very forcefully on this kind of candour in general terms, long before she published Sartre's letters; but, after their publication, the personal application of her words seems evident:

> If two speakers convince each other that they dominate events and people about whom they exchange confidences, on the pretext of practising sincerity, they are deceiving themselves. There is a kind of honesty I have often noted which is nothing but flagrant hypocrisy; confined to the realm of sexuality, it does not aim in the least to create an intimate understanding between a man and a woman, but to provide one of them — most often the man — with a facile alibi: he cherishes the delusion that, by confessing his infidelities, he atones for them, when in fact he is inflicting a double violence on his partner.[9]

It is plain, then, that total candour could be not only fundamentally insincere but a source of pain.

Sartre, in his novel, *L'Age de raison*, set in 1938 and written in 1939, is also concerned with the theme of utter sincerity between lovers engaged in a lengthy liaison: Mathieu, a projection of Sartre himself, and his mistress, the overweight and miserable Marcelle. The noted authority on Sartre's work, Michel Contat, perceptively observed of Marcelle: 'She is so obviously the opposite of Simone de Beauvoir — whose place she fills in the constellation of roles surrounding the hero — that one wonders if Sartre did not make his companion unrecognisable in order to settle accounts with her just the same, whether unconsciously or not'.[10] Mathieu and Marcelle — just like Sartre and Simone de Beauvoir — have made a pact to tell all but, as the author of *Le Deuxième Sexe* was to remark about these fictional characters, in pretending to do so they manage to say nothing: 'Words are sometimes merely a more skilful way of keeping quiet than if one were silent'.[11] We know that she offered some criticism about

Marcelle to Sartre, but not its purport. In the autobiography, she gives little away on this subject. The difference between Sartre and his creation, Mathieu, is, however, a vital one. Mathieu utters the fateful words that are true, at least for the moment for him: he tells Marcelle that he no longer loves her. Not surprisingly, she throws him out. Mathieu reflects that he is a swine (*salaud*), of the sort who people Sartre's work, and afterwards he is sorry, because 'it was to her alone that he could talk about his life, his fears, his hopes . . . . I have abandoned Marcelle *for nothing*'.[12] The situation might have been saved if Mathieu had not yielded to his notion of total candour, if he had taken the precaution of letting some time elapse so that 'words may lose their efficacity', as Simone de Beauvior put it in her autobiography.[13] It is a theme to which she would return in her own novels.

As for Sartre, he stressed Mathieu's guilt in an interview given in 1945, when *L'Age de raison* was published. Mathieu's fault lay in 'his loveless commitment eight years before. Or rather, Mathieu is not truly committed to Marcelle . . . because he knew that this liaison was not a joint undertaking. They see each other four times a week. They say that they tell each other everything: in reality, they never stop lying, because their relationship is false and deceptive'.[14] It is a heavily darkened version of a bond similar to that between himself and Simone de Beauvoir.

Doubtless there is considerable risk in interpreting life through fiction, yet equally it would be mistaken to disregard the contribution that fiction can make to understanding, provided it is treated with discretion. That there is such a connection here is plain from remarks made by both writers. Their novels are not highly imaginative and inventive, but are deeply rooted in their own emotional dilemmas and actual experiences. As Sartre himself wrote to Simone de Beauvoir in a letter of 10 May 1940: ' . . . we have *put* ourselves in our novels'. Speaking of her novel, *L'Invitée*, as well as of his own *L'Age de raison*, he added: 'we display ourselves, we speak of each other, of our little affairs, of the sort of people we love . . . we are defenceless — . . .'.[15] These words of his cannot be overlooked, even though he stated also with greater nuance that her fictional characters are 'you and not you' (and the same applies to his own).

In old age, Sartre made a devastating admission to Olivier Todd, a journalist and writer whom he knew well and who was married to the daughter of his late friend, Paul Nizan. Olivier Todd asked Sartre how he managed to keep so many affairs with women going at once. 'I lie to them', said Sartre. 'It is simpler and more straightforward.' Olivier Todd was surprised: 'You lie to all of them?' Sartre smiled: 'To all of them'. Then came the vital query: 'Even to *le Castor*?' Sartre replied: 'Above all to *le Castor*'.[16] In one brief answer, Sartre had destroyed the edifice, so carefully constructed in her autobiography. He had challenged the impression she gives that theirs was a unique relationship, as it were a tree rooted in truth and plain-dealing even if occasionally shaken by passing storms. Here was Sartre saying that it was special only in that he lied to her more than to any of his other women. In vain did Olivier Todd say agreeable things about Simone de Beauvoir in his book, *Un Fils rebelle*. She never forgave him, and could scarcely mention his name without an expression of savage contempt.

All this is to consider the liaison in its entirety over a long period. In the beginning, during the relatively brief period of her complete union with Sartre, around 1930–1, she lapsed into wifely domesticity and dwindled into 'the little woman'. As a girl she had always wanted to be allied to a superior man, and in Sartre she felt she had found this paragon. It was not just that she regarded him as being cleverer than herself (had she not come second to him in the examination?): he was always full of new ideas and theories, and she felt — rightly — that he was more of a philosopher and more creative than she was. Sartre was not at all gratified by her dependence on him — husbandly responsibility did not figure in his plans. This period of dependence was one she would never forget. It was to be translated into her novels and given to several of her feminine characters who become totally subservient to their husbands or lovers, only to find themselves in a rut of falsehood or false happiness, or abandoned when they reach their forties for a younger woman.

Meanwhile, she discovered that Sartre was still seeing Simone-Camille Sans (known on the stage as Camille), who had been his mistress before his union with the future author of *L'Invitée*. Of stunning beauty, free-living and totally amoral (she had had many escapades and lovers in her native Toulouse), Camille was also extremely talented. She became the mistress of the famous actor-manager, Charles Dullin, and later his wife. It was through her and her connection with Dullin that Sartre gained experience of the theatre, which also plays so important a part in the setting of *L'Invitée* and the occupation of its leading characters.

Camille herself appears in the autobiography as a dangerous rival. Family poverty had not enabled Simone de Beauvoir to dress well; she was only too aware of her rather shabby appearance as a girl; and in her early bohemian days with Sartre she was usually to be found inexpensively dressed in black. Here was the dazzling young Camille with her exotic taste in men, clothes and décor, already successful, and appearing as an actress in her own play. Her beauty, her freedom, her gifts, aroused Simone de Beauvoir's envy. It was only in later life that as a writer she was able to have her revenge, by revealing how pleased Camille was at the opportunity for greater advancement in the theatre provided by the removal of the Jews during the German Occupation; and by a horrific account of the actress's decline into drunkenness in old age and her lonely and sordid death.

The appointment of Simone de Beauvoir to a teaching post in Marseilles in the spring of 1931 put an end to her period of domestic submission and dependence on Sartre. He had been appointed to a post in Le Havre. They would be at opposite ends of the country. Sartre proposed marriage, which would allow them to seek permission to teach in the same place, but she declined the offer. Apparently, it was not renewed, although he later proposed at various times to several different women with whom he was in love, if circumstances seemed to him to demand it.

She always regarded her months in Marseilles as a turning-point, for there she was not only earning her own living, she was also forced to rely on her own inner resources. This was the time when she took to making long expeditions on foot and alone into the mountains. Her colleagues warned her of the risks, but were disregarded. She had loved the countryside ever since she was a girl, and her descriptions of nature represent one of the most attractive, evocative and lyrical aspects of her writing. As for Sartre, he never shared her passion for 'chlorophyl', or fresh air, and he would speak ironically to his women friends about this need of hers to commune with nature.

In the summer of 1932, Simone de Beauvoir was appointed to a position at the *lyceé* in Rouen, and so she and Sartre, at nearby Le Havre, could see more of each other. They spent holidays in Spain and Spanish Morocco, and in the following year they went first to England and later to Italy together. However, Sartre was soon making full use of the freedom granted in their contract. In September 1933, when he went to the Institut Français in Berlin to pursue research, he fell in love with the wife of one of his colleagues, 'Marie Girard'. He had known her since his days at the Ecole Normale Supérieure. This was the first of Sartre's passionate or 'serious' affairs, as distinct from his passing fancies, since the formulation of the 'arrangement'. Simone de Beauvoir became so worried that she contrived to obtain a medical certificate for leave of absence on the pretext of nervous exhaustion, and left for Berlin. Once there, she was soon involved in the usual discussions and travels with Sartre. She met 'Marie Girard': 'I liked her and did not feel any jealousy towards her', she would relate in her autobiography, while admitting that jealousy was not an emotion foreign to her.[17] It may be doubted whether she was quite so Olympian at the time.

The partners must have felt that something was missing from their relationship, or they would not have taken the strange course they did. They chose to 'adopt' one of Simone de Beauvoir's pupils. This was Olga Kosakiewicz (later the actress, Olga Dominique). Olga's father was a Russian nobleman, her mother was French, and at the time of the Bolshevik Revolution they had taken refuge in France. The girl appeared vulnerable yet truly 'modern": she detested anything bourgeois; her responses seemed idiosyncratic, fresh and original; above all, she was endowed with the great virtue of 'authenticity'. She deeply admired Simone de Beauvoir who was much taken with her Slav generosity and her independent spirit. As for Sartre, ever attracted to youth, he complicated matters by falling in love with the pale, fair-haired Russian girl. He would tend to get involved with a number of Simone de Beauvoir's pupils, who were often inclined to have a 'crush' on her. From being teachers entrusted by Olga's parents with supervising her studies, the two companions became engaged in the formation of what they called a 'trio'. Emotional pressures built up in the confined provincial atmosphere (visits to Paris were rare and brief). Only the cult of youth and the desire to forge new human relationships or 'to create man anew' could have led them into an imbroglio whose highly charged character might seem inevitable in terms of common sense. The triangle, after all, with its inescapable complications, has long served as a basic pattern in novels and dramas. This would not be the last time that the two supreme rationalists would plunge deliberately into a course of conduct contrary to reason.

It was Sartre who changed the nature of the 'trio' by his obsession with Olga. He would sit with Simone de Beauvoir, questioning the significance of the girl's every expression or gesture. Naturally, his companion felt pained. She was also irritated by Olga's growing animosity towards her, and she was upset by her own disagreements with Sartre. Besides, she could not help being led to query the very basis of their special relationship:

> I owned to myself that it was wrong to mistake another person for myself under that equivocal, all-too-convenient word: "we". These were experiences which each person lived on his own account; I had always maintained that words fail to convey the veritable presence of reality: I had to draw the consequences of this. I was cheating when I said: "We are one". Harmony between two individuals is never given, it must always go on being conquered,

she mused in *La Force de l'âge* about her feelings at the time.[18] She saw that Sartre was experiencing excitement, worry, anger, delight of a kind 'that he did not know with me. The disquiet I felt at this went further than jealousy: at times I wondered whether my happiness was not resting entirely on a huge lie', she reflected in her autobiography.

The nagging suspicion about the value of the word 'we' in connection with their personal relationship did not extend, however, to their general views. She went on relating their opinions and reactions in the first person plural as if the partners, notwithstanding any private differences or upsets, were always fundamentally at one. She liked to write, for instance, that: 'we never imagined'; 'we never seriously questioned'; 'we thought man should be created anew'; 'we smiled at this expression'; 'we were usually carried along by a current'; 'we invented attitudes, theories, ideas'.[19] This frequent use of the word 'we' — almost the royal 'we' — ends by imposing upon the reader a sense of the couple's total intellectual and emotional unity and understanding. This impression predominates and, as it were, covers any candid account of questioning about dangerous tensions.

The period of doubt engendered by the 'trio' served as the catalyst for her novel, *L'Invitée*, dedicated to Olga Kosakiewicz. There, the triangle, whose every subtle nuance of emotion and attitude is thoroughly probed, finally dissolves when Françoise chooses to turn on the gas which will suffocate the sleeping Xavière. This murderous gesture, however unconvincing in the book, given the character of Françoise, is for Simone de Beauvoir as novelist the only logical way out of a poisonous situation. In actuality, and less melodramatically, it was Olga who, torn and suffering in her turn from the pressures exerted on her by the partners, put an end to it by taking up with Sartre's pupil, Jacques-Laurent Bost (whom she later married).

What Simone de Beauvoir does not relate in her memoirs, though the episode figures in fictional form in the relationship between Françoise and Gerbert in *L'Invitée*, is her own affair with Jacques-Laurent Bost. After Simone de Beauvoir had recovered from a serious attack of pneumonia (also given to Françoise in the novel) early in 1937, she had gone to convalesce in the South of France. She was then accompanied on a walking tour by Bost. When told that they had become lovers, Sartre did not disapprove in the least. 'It happened exactly as in *L'Invitée*', Simone de Beauvoir was to inform her joint biographers, Claude Francis and Fernande Gontier.[20] A new trio took shape when Sartre, Simone de Beauvoir and Jacques-Laurent Bost went on holiday to Greece together. Later that summer, Simone de Beauvoir took Olga on a walking tour of Alsace: the girl had felt annoyed at being left out of the visit to Greece. The only person who was not told about Simone de Beauvoir's involvement with Bost was Olga, thought to be insufficiently strong to bear the strain of so much candour. Henceforward, both Olga and Bost would remain part of the select group or court around Sartre and Simone de Beauvoir, known as 'the family', whose members often received financial support from the 'parental' companions. Apparently, the relationship of *le Castor* with Bost continued until after the 1939–45 War when it was transmuted into friendship.

An episode less well documented than the 'trio' with Olga, a bond whose torments are translated into those of the condemned threesome in Sartre's play, *Huis-Clos*, concerns the question of abortion. Simone de Beauvoir was to admit under oath that she had had an abortion:[21] this was many years later, in 1973, during the agitation in France for the repeal of the anti-abortion law, in which she played an influential role. The respective responses of Mathieu and his pregnant mistress Marcelle to the matter of abortion provide one of the central themes of Sartre's *L'Age de raison*. Now this theme can be seen as yet another link in the chain that binds fictional personage to model. Speaking in 1945, Sartre observed that '[people] were upset because *L'Age de raison* turned on an affair of abortion. Quite wrongly. The fact is that in 1938 abortion was treated as a criminal offence: therefore it existed. Why choose to close one's eyes to it . . . ?'[22] Simone de Beauvoir has the heroine of her novel, *Le Sang des autres*, undergo an abortion, depicted in grim detail. But in her autobiography she was not likely to allude to any involvement of her own at a time when abortion was a matter for the police. She could perhaps have discussed it in the last volume of her memoirs, *Tout compte fait*, published in 1972, when she helped to found a movement to assist women accused of abortion, but she did not choose to do so.

Sartre himself continued to confess to her his affairs with other women, and what he called his 'petites histoires'.[23] Once, when Merleau-Ponty asked Sartre about his relations with Simone de Beauvoir, he (Sartre) informed her of his reply: 'I told him what you thought, that it was settled once and for all and on such a plane that we were not bothered by my little springtime episodes' ('mes petites histoires de printemps').[24] Here was a use of the word 'we' perhaps even more commandingly imperialistic than that of Simone de Beauvoir. By 'we were not bothered' he meant that he himself was not overly troubled by these episodes or by their effect on her, which she possibly underplayed in order to preserve their union. He must have gleaned some pleasure from telling her about them 'while blowing smoke from my pipe in your face and watching the effect they have on your dear little mug', as he graciously put it.[25]

Olga had been supplanted by her younger sister, Wanda, who would also remain a member of 'the family'. (As the actress Marie Olivier, Wanda was to play leading roles in his plays from *Les Mains sales* to *Les Séquestrés d'Altona*.) In May 1940, despite the pain it might inflict on his companion, Sartre reluctantly proposed marriage to the girl. He had been mobilised; and marriage seemed the only way to obtain leave to see her when she was terrified of having contracted tuberculosis. Once, he had even torn up some letters that Simone de Beauvoir had written to him, letters which she had expressly asked him to keep, and which could have served as notes for her writings. The reason he gave was that he was sharing a room with Wanda who moved about in it while he slept, and he did not want her to see them. True, he *told* Simone de Beauvoir that he had destroyed them, but what could have been a more wounding offence to a writer of her gravity and ambition?

At the same time as he was engaged in his tumultuous affair with Wanda, Sartre was expressing his passion for 'Louise Védrine', a Polish-Jewish pupil of Simone de Beauvoir's, a girl deeply attached to her. This interlude or new trio was brought to an end by the outbreak of war, when 'Louise Védrine' left the country with her parents. Nor should one forget others on whom he focused his attentions, including 'Lucile', one of Charles Dullin's pupils. Simone de Beauvoir knew about them all; she continued to be repeatedly assured of her unique place, of his need for her, and of his deep affection, in fine phrases; yet she would have to share the brief eight days of his leave with Wanda.

Free and novel liaison or not, it is difficult to see how this situation may be said to differ greatly from that of the complaisant wife, who retains her position and status in the eyes of the world despite her husband's philandering, and whose own affairs are viewed with complacency or indifference by her spouse. Sartre could assure her that a liaison was more valuable and entailed more responsibilities than marriage, but he himself gave little proof of responsibility. All was to be covered by words. What is at stake here is the question of loyalty: it seems plain that Sartre's interpretation of this differed from the meaning usually attached to the concept. Their favourite password was 'Cynara', after the title of the once well-known American film with Kay Francis, with its quotation: 'I have been faithful to thee, Cynara! in my fashion', a line taken from a poem by Ernest Dowson. Indeed, that sort of *fin de siècle* cynicism fits their attitude well, rather than the high tone of unique freedom with which she tried to endow their relationship in her autobiography and her interviews. At the same time, however, she managed skilfully to suggest its difficulties and limitations, as well as the pain inflicted not only on her but on those 'contingent' lovers who mistakenly thought that they were entitled to a deeper and more lasting commitment than they received from Sartre or from herself. Whether consciously or not, she provided much of the material which suggests a less elevated image of their liaison.

More strikingly, their relationship had another dimension. As intellectual partners, their union appears remarkable: it is not common to find two important writers of different gender so intimately linked over so long a period in intellectual exchange, each so closely attuned to the literary wishes, intentions and aspirations of the other. Olivier Todd, who met them in later years, spoke of 'their incomparable complicity'. And he went on:

> They seemed to think simultaneously. . . . They moved into gear, they whisked along, overlapping, in a way I have never seen in any other couple. This brother–sister Siamese twinship could be a bit awe-inspiring. Every time I saw them together my astonishment would be renewed. Simone de Beauvoir was likely to finish a sentence that Sartre had begun, and vice versa. There was even a kind of mimicry in their hoarse voices. In his views Sartre was bolder than she was. Almost always he ended by carrying *le Castor* along with him. She often kept quiet because he was inclined to monopolise the conversation, in *macho* style. Besides, what need was there for her to break in, since she recognised her own voice in his? Impressive. And equally touching was their way of addressing each other formally as 'vous' right up to Sartre's death.[26]

In public they never spoke to each other or about each other in a familiar or intimate way: he was always 'Sartre' when she was discussing him in her work or in the interviews she gave later in her career.

Anyone who saw the film *Sartre par lui-même*, in which she participated, will be able to confirm the veracity of Olivier Todd's observations. The companions functioned in this 'overlapping' way not unlike many a long-lived and closely married couple, where one partner instinctively knows what the other is thinking, where both often simultaneously think the same thing. More rare, perhaps, is a union in the diverse fields of literature, philosophy and politics, a marriage of minds of the kind enjoyed by Sartre and Simone de Beauvoir as writers.

Within this intellectual union, it was she who would provide certain wifely domestic services in the early years (from the very first, he asked her to take his washing to the laundry). She took a motherly interest in his well-being, scolding him for not wearing a hat under the Moroccan sun, or later, when he was ill, diluting his whisky. She reprimanded him when he behaved shabbily to 'Martine Bourdin', and he expressed contrition like a naughty child to his mother or acknowledged 'judge' — 'everything decent in me is due to you', he told her.[27] According to his one-time secretary, Jean Cau, she was not only his first disciple but a kind of possessive and domineering mother. Doubtless, Sartre could be irritated by her supervision while at the same time he needed her care and support, and he could always count on them. No wonder that at the end of ten years he was happy to renew their 'arrangement' or, as he called it, their 'morganatic marriage'. He once remarked: 'In a certain sense, . . . I owe her everything'. With commendable hyperbole he told her: 'Everything I think or feel or write is for you'.[28] (All the same, L'Age de raison, for instance, was dedicated to Wanda Kosakiewicz.)

Both partners loved gossip, discussing their friends and acquaintances, analysing their motives and conduct. All this would prove immensely useful to both of them for their writings. She was ready to accept his philosophical theories, adopting the very phraseology in which he expressed his thought (and later on, she concurred with his political views). The Sartrian existentialist vocabulary — 'the Other', 'authenticity', 'contingency', 'in situation', 'to take on responsibility', and so forth — became an essential part of her language too. He would even leave it to her to publish polemical articles (for instance, the attack on a former associate — 'Merleau-Ponty et le pseudo-sartrisme') which he did not want to write himself.

It was Sartre who encouraged her to get on with writing a novel in the early years of their association. He accused her of timidity, and he advised her to put more of herself into her work. 'I should never dare!', she exclaimed, afraid of the risk of compromising herself so deeply. 'Dare!', counselled Sartre.[29] How many budding women writers of the day could have done with a knowledgeable adviser who would not only urge them to take risks but show them how to do so? Sartre's advice to her was invaluable; and so was hers to him. He admitted that he learned something from her novelistic technique.

They became severe critics of each other's work. She told him that *La Nausée* needed more 'suspense' in it and that he employed too many adjectives and similes. Usually, Sartre propounded a 'theory'; she criticised it, suggested nuances, sometimes rejected it or proposed that he revise it, which he sometimes did. He conveyed to her all the main ideas of his important philosophical work, *L'Etre et le Néant*, as he was formulating them, before it was written.

In his view, it was not just that she knew as much about philosophy as he did: he would declare that

> she was the only one who was on my level of understanding of myself, of what I wanted to do. So she was the perfect person . . . with whom to engage in dialogue. . . . It is a unique grace. Probably there are many writers, men or women, who have been loved and helped by someone very intelligent. . . . What is unique with Simone de Beauvoir and myself is this relationship of equality.[30]

Sartre agreed that they each relied on the other's judgment, waiting for the other's seal of approval, ever since he wrote *La Nausée*. According to him, when engaged in mutual criticism they even shouted at each other and descended to insults, but he ended by accepting most of her critical observations. And he was equally severe with her work — 'the maximum of severity. There is no sense in making critical remarks which are not severe when one has the good fortune to love the man or woman one is criticising'.[31] He was surely right in speaking of such an intellectual partnership as 'a unique grace'.

If he regarded her as an 'intimate friend' together with his close male comrades, he also saw her in traditional terms as masculine through her intellect. Notwithstanding his remarks about a 'relationship of equality', he had inherited the view that the intellect is a masculine domain. Thus he could employ words not very different from those used about Mme de Staël or George Sand by their contemporaries: 'The marvellous thing with Simone de Beauvoir is that she has the intelligence of a man . . . and the sensibility of a woman'.[32] His words imply that a woman of intellect must share the qualities of a man.

Their intellectual union would not remain solely in the realms of philosophy and literature. It would be coloured by their political attitudes as well. Their views on political issues were largely to be in harmony until Sartre's very last years, when they began to diverge. How two pleasure-loving *littérateurs* and bohemian anarchists became committed radicals and self-appointed ambassadors of the Left, was the consequence of catastrophic events in Europe which left none of their generation unscathed.

Notes

1. *L'Invitée*, Gallimard, 1943, p. 27.
2. Jean-Paul Sartre, *Lettres au Castor et à quelques autres 1926–1939*, Gallimard, 1983, vol. 1, pp. 149, 166, 290, 330, 486.
3. Raymond Aron, *Mémoires*, Julliard, 1983, p. 38.
4. *Mémoires d'une jeune fille rangée*, p. 338.
5. Douglas Johnson, review of the film, *Sartre par lui-même*, *The Times Literary Supplement*, 12 November 1976.
6. *La Cérémonie des Adieux, suivi de Entretiens avec Jean-Paul Sartre*, Gallimard, 1981, p. 378.
7. *La Force de l'âge*, Gallimard, 1960, pp. 27–8.
8. Ibid., p. 371 and note 1 (original emphasis).
9. Ibid., p. 29.
10. Michel Contat, 'Avec Sartre à Montparnasse', *Le Monde*, 15 August 1986.
11. *La Force de l'âge*, p. 29.
12. Jean-Paul Sartre, *L'Age de raison*, Gallimard (1943) 1945, pp. 306–7.
13. *La Force de l'âge*, p. 29.
14. Jean-Paul Sartre, interview with Christian Grisoli, October 1945, in M. Contat and M. Rybalka, *Les Ecrits de Sartre*, Gallimard, 1970, p. 115.
15. Sartre, *Lettres au Castor et à quelques autres 1940–1963*, Gallimard, vol. 2, p. 217.
16. Olivier Todd, *Un Fils rebelle*, Grasset, 1981, p. 117.
17. *La Force de l'âge*, p. 191.
18. Ibid., p. 268.
19. Ibid., pp. 297, 370–1.
20. C. Francis and F. Gontier, *Simone de Beauvoir*, p. 176 and note.
21. 'Déposition de Simone de Beauvoir au procès de Bobigny', in C.

Francis and F. Gontier, *Les Ecrits de Simone de Beauvoir*, Gallimard, 1979, p. 513.

22. Sartre, interview with Christian Grisoli, October 1945, in M. Contat and M. Rybalka, *Les Ecrits de Sartre*, p. 115.
23. Sartre, *Lettres au Castor*, vol. 1, p. 144.
24. Ibid., p. 192.
25. Ibid., p. 144.
26. Olivier Todd, *Un Fils rebelle*, p. 106.
27. Sartre, *Lettres au Castor*, vol. 1, p. 359.
28. Ibid., pp. 336, 380; interview with Madeleine Gobeil (1965), quoted by C. Francis and F. Gontier, *Les Ecrits de Simone de Beauvoir*, p. 20.
29. *La Force de l'âge*, pp. 323–4.
30. Sartre, 'Autoportrait a soixante-dix ans', in idem, *Situations*, volume X, Gallimard, 1976, p. 190.
31. Ibid., p. 191.
32. Sartre, interview with Madeleine Gobeil (1965), quoted in *Les Ecrits de Simone de Beauvoir*, p. 20.

4 The Story of a Conversion

The second volume of Simone de Beauvoir's autobiography, *La Force de l'âge*, tells — among other things — the tale of a conversion. This change of heart is purely secular, a movement not from the Rightist opinions of her father that she echoed as a girl, but from highly stressed indifference or self-deception in political matters to commitment. It is a conversion that she perceives in strictly moral terms, and one that ultimately was to function as a replacement for the intense but now lost Catholicism of her childhood.

This journey, which is carefully and repeatedly signposted in the book, takes her through the major crises and upheavals of the period: the Great Depression of 1929; Hitler's phenomenal rise to power in Germany and the growing miasma of Nazism; the unsettled era of the Left coalition or Popular Front government in France and the spread of Fascist movements there; the Spanish Civil War (that 'last great cause'); the dread Soviet purges and the Moscow show trials of old Bolsheviks; the disastrous Fall of France in 1940 and the bitter years of German Occupation; right up to the Liberation of Paris in 1944. It is the tale of her slow awakening to social responsibility, recounted as being parallel to that of Sartre, although he is sometimes shown as being further along the road to commitment than she is herself. This volume of the autobiography is thus built upon self-reproach: the pained recollection that it was not she but others who were struggling against Fascism and Nazism in the 1930s, or fighting for the Spanish Republic; and suffering persecution, exile, degradation, torture, death. This strategy of self-criticism served a particular purpose.

The stress is placed at first on her pacifism and anti-militarism in the 1930s. Here, she was by no means alone. The battles of the 1914–18 War that had scarred French soil, the huge losses sustained by the French in that holocaust, turned many of her compatriots against the very notion of another conflict with Germany. Simone de Beauvoir satirised her own patriotic militarism as a child during the First World War in *Mémoires d'une jeune fille rangée.* For her, nationalism was permanently associated with her father's Rightist viewpoint, and it seemed to her as to many of her fellow citizens that anything was preferable to the horrors of another war which (all were agreed) would inevitably prove to be even worse than its predecessor.

Ignorance, so she relates, made both Sartre and herself share the optimism of the French Left which saw the economic crisis of 1929 as a sign of the imminent demise of capitalism. Of one thing they were sure: they were against society in its present form. Their feeling that it was totally corrupt and rotten was not based on analysis. According to her, both of them were supremely bored by political affairs at that period in the early 1930s. And this state of mind continued as far as she was concerned. Changes of ministry (of which there were many), debates in the Chambre des députés — all this seemed utterly futile. Consequently, she would remain supremely indifferent to the struggle for votes for women, led by Louise Weiss. The contempt that Simone de Beauvoir felt for the (often shady) political manoeuvring under the Third Republic, would never vary, and this scorn would extend to parliamentary democracy as a whole, for whose values she never expressed the slightest understanding or respect. It is significant that this scorn and loathing for parliamentary democracy was shared not only by adherents of the extreme Left, but by those on the extreme Right also.

The fact that Simone de Beauvoir as well as Sartre saw themselves as writers and intellectuals first and foremost, with a prime commitment to literature, meant that everything else had to be subordinated to this aim. Both of them, she felt, were close to the anarchists — in fact, it would seem, to that generalised anarchy often favoured by apolitical artists and writers. Their stance, indeed, had something in common with that of the Surrealists, who then formed the most influential movement in literature and the arts. Like the Surrealists, they welcomed the idea of revolution as an end in itself; though, unlike Aragon and Eluard, they did not ally themselves with the Communist Party or sing the praises of Stalin.

As for the Socialist Party, which Sartre's friend at the Ecole Normale Supérieure, Raymond Aron, that lifelong pragmatist, had joined, they despised it because they saw it as 'tainted' by the bourgeoisie and 'because our temperaments were averse to reformism:

society could only change globally, at one blow, through a violent convulsion'.[1] They showed no concern for what was to replace the existing arrangement once it was destroyed, and for the human losses likely to ensue in a violent overthrow. This visceral commitment to change through violent upheaval (shared by anarchists, Dadaists, Futurists, Surrealists) would remain an enduring tenet of theirs even after they became politically committed.

In this area of gut reaction, then, there is really no need for Simone de Beauvoir to present her progress as a conversion. For there were some psychological or 'temperamental' elements that survived unchanged. It may be said, therefore, that her careful presentation of her developing views as a conversion is somewhat overdramatised. Long before the heralded alteration in her standpoint, she detested capitalism and existing society, and she sympathised with the proletariat as a generalised entity rather than as a body made up of individual human beings with whom one could enter into contact. She was contemptuous of parliamentary democracy, hostile to reformism and eager for world revolution 'at one blow'. Apolitical or not, she herself admits that her sympathies, like Sartre's, lay unwaveringly on the Left.

Inevitably such views, however 'unscientific', led them towards the Communists, who were then seen as being heroically in the forefront of the battle against Fascism and Nazism. The Soviet Union thus amassed a great deal of sympathy. The companions might well be fascinated by jazz and American films, and influenced by the novels of William Faulkner and John Dos Passos; but, indifferent as they were to the structure of democracy, for them the United States spelt above all capitalism, exploitation, unemployment, lynchings and oppression of the Blacks. They shared their distaste for the United States in general with their fellow-countrymen on the Right whom they detested. From this simplistic view they would never waver (even after some personal experience later acquired through visiting the United States after the 1939–45 War). Here again, the placing of their sympathies with the Soviet Union remained unchanged both before and after the notorious Hitler–Stalin Pact of August 1939, which would lead Sartre's Communist friend, the novelist Paul Nizan, to break with the Party and to be vilified by his erstwhile comrades. In time, the shock that the companions felt at the (revealing) alliance between the two totalitarian states would be followed by excuses for Stalin.

Simone de Beauvoir makes it clear that it was Sartre alone who was vaguely tempted (at various times while she was teaching at Rouen in the early 1930s) to participate in the revolution, throw in his lot with the workers' struggle and join the Communist Party. The 'provisional' decision they reached, however, she presents as a joint one. The argument runs as follows: if they were members of the proletariat, the struggle would have been their own, and necessarily they would have had to join the Communist Party. Still, while the workers' struggle 'was a matter of concern to us, it was not our own: all that could be required of us was that we always side with it [the proletariat]. We had to pursue our own undertakings which were not at one with joining the Party'.[2] This use of the word 'we' blurs the issue: for if it was Sartre and not herself who thought of joining the Communist Party, why is her opinion on not doing so presented as being the same as his? Was it she who persuaded him to hold back?

One of Simone de Beauvoir's closest friends and colleagues at Rouen was Colette Audry, who belonged to a Trotskyist group and who was acquainted with one of the leaders of the Left opposition to Stalin, the Russian-born writer, Boris Souvarine. Brought up in France, he was among the founders of the French Communist Party. He had defended Trotsky against Stalin as early as 1924, and as a result he had been expelled from the Comintern and from the French Communist Party he had helped to found. Souvarine's revelations about Stalin's tyranny, familiar to the initiated, were possibly known to the companions through Colette Audry. However, they seem to have been indifferent to such matters. They showed a similar lack of interest, so Simone de Beauvoir relates, in the case of Victor Serge, the novelist and lifelong revolutionary activist, who was banished to Central Asia with other members of the Left opposition to Stalin, many of whom perished there. Victor Serge only survived through the campaign to obtain his release which was led by French writers like André Gide and André Malraux, authors whom Sartre admired at that period. Nor would the companions be moved by André Gide's volte-face on Stalin's Russia, and his revelations about the shortcomings of the Soviet regime in his *Retour de l'U R S S*. They did not take the book seriously, declared Simone de Beauvoir.

Stalin's purges and the Moscow show trials elicited from her a response that would recur all too often throughout her life whenever something unpleasant would be revealed, not just about the Soviet system but about other later 'revolutionary' regimes for which she expressed sympathy and admiration. 'But what did the trials that were taking place in Moscow mean?', she enquired ingenuously in *La Force de l'âge*. And she went on: 'We had never imagined the USSR to be a paradise, but neither had we seriously questioned the building of socialism. It was embarrassing to be prompted to do so at a time when the policy of the democracies [towards the Spanish Republic] made us sick. Was there no longer a corner of the world to which hope could cling?'[3] This yearning to be able to fix one's hopes on some great good place somewhere indicates how religious aspiration has been transferred from a divine source to a political surface.

Moreover, her rhetorical question concerning the 'meaning' of the Moscow trials did not lead her to engage in any effort to discover the truth, although plenty of evidence was by then becoming readily available. She did not apparently desire to probe too deeply into a phenomenon that would necessarily undermine her grounds for hope. Her total rejection of the French Socialist Party itself did not preclude either the belief in a generalised socialism (undefined) or the hopeful assumption that socialism was being built in the Soviet Union. Such faith in the word 'socialism' as in the word 'revolution' was to linger long in Simone de Beauvoir's world view, and it clearly antedated the much heralded climactic moment of her conversion to social responsibility as described in her memoirs.

On Hitler's rise to power, she frankly owns that she remained comparatively sanguine. All of Sartre's letters to her from Germany, written when he was at the Institut Français in Berlin (1933–4) have been lost, according to her note in his *Lettres au Castor*. She herself does not say much about Nazism in her account of the two visits she paid to Sartre in Germany in 1934. Her list of political developments there (as elsewhere) is taken from her researches into the newspaper archives, researches undertaken at the time of writing *La Force de l'âge*. It possibly conveys a false picture of the facts of which she herself was aware during her visits (and after). Superficially, Berlin did not give her the impression of being under the heel of a ruthless dictator. As for Sartre, he associated there chiefly with intellectuals, and he would later speak of his anti-Nazism, 'at least in my head'.[4] For her part, she admits their 'fairly considerable equanimity', 'a comparative equanimity' shared in her view by the French Left as a whole, where Nazi moves against intellectuals and artists as well as anti-Semitic measures were concerned.[5] The activities of the French Fascist movements (which nearly brought down the government in February 1934) did not apparently move the companions unduly. They disapproved, but they did not really face the threat of Fascism and Nazism, according to Simone de Beauvoir, when speaking of the Left as a whole and as it were including Sartre and herself within it, despite their non-involvement.

It was not until some years later, just before the outbreak of War in 1939, that the press revealed the existence of the concentration camp at Dachau, and that her pupil, Bianca Bienenfeld, who had relatives in Vienna, told her in detail acquired at first-hand about the persecution of the Jews. After that, Simone de Beauvoir realised that her broad attitude to the Jews, inherited from one branch of the eighteenth-century Enlightenment, namely her opinion that 'Jews don't exist: there are only men', could not be sustained in the face of their persecution as Jews by the Nazis.[6]

As for the left-wing causes of the 1930s, and notably the Popular Front government which came to power in France in 1936, the companions with their Leftist tinge sympathised with it from a distance. Sartre himself was to confirm her account of their attitude. They were stirred by popular marches, but they remained 'spectators'.[7] When the Popular Front government under Léon Blum failed to intervene in favour of the Spanish Republic, their enthusiasm turned to indignation and anger. People they knew, like that extreme idealist, Simone Weil, went off to serve on the Republican side. The companions felt powerless; they were not impelled to 'act' by signing manifestos or joining in demonstrations, as did many of their contemporaries: they reacted emotionally in private.

From 1936, Simone de Beauvoir was teaching in Paris at the Lycée Molière. This move was regarded as promotion after

Rouen. Her new pupils were astonished by her appearance when she arrived to take her first class. She came in wearing a lilac-coloured silk blouse and a pleated skirt — young-looking, heavily made-up, and carrying a copy of the women's magazine, *Marie-Claire*. One of her pupils would recall how Simone de Beauvoir spoke fluently, without notes, in a hoarse voice. The girls struggled to understand what she was saying about Husserl and phenomenology, struck by 'the dazzling virtuosity of her mind which intimidated us a good deal'.[8] There seems little doubt that Simone de Beauvoir could prove an extremely attractive role model to her students, and that some of them (Olga Kosakiewicz, Nathalie Sorokine, 'Louise Védrine' and others) became overly attached to her. That this influence might possibly be exerted consciously is suggested through the character of the teacher Chantal, viewed with irony in *Quand prime le spirituel*; and there is a hint of Muriel Spark's Miss Brodie, in her prime, about it.

The return to Paris meant a return to old haunts. Simone de Beauvoir was born in Montparnasse: now she made her head-quarters in Le Dôme, close by her birthplace, where she would sit writing at one of the café's tables. She had taken a room in a hotel in the noisy rue de la Gaîté, near the much loved Bobino music-hall and the Théâtre Montparnasse. With her friends she liked to frequent Le Jockey and lesser-known jazz dives and dance-halls favoured by Blacks, haunts that would figure in *L'Invitée*. It was only in 1938 that she began to spend evenings in Saint-Germain-des-Prés, in the café de Flore, then the resort of people who worked in the cinema and the theatre.

With the crisis over the Sudeten Germans in Czechoslovakia it looked as if war with Hitler could not be avoided after all. At the time of the Munich agreement of September 1938, when France and England abandoned Czechoslovakia to its fate, many people, including Simone de Beauvoir, breathed a loud sigh of relief. She felt that anything, 'even the most cruel injustice', was preferable to another war. Sartre could not agree with her: 'We can't go on indefinitely giving in to Hitler', he told her, although he was not sorry to see the threat of war averted.[9]

According to her own account, she finally realised that war was inevitable early in 1939. She could no longer close her eyes to the barbarous atrocities committed by the Nazis, convinced as she was by Sartre that support for appeasement turned them both into accomplices of the persecutors. Besides, she felt guilty: she had not 'lifted a finger' to stop it — as if, by joining in all the left-wing protest marches, she would have had any more effect in halting evil than those well-meaning people who did participate in them. What such participation would have meant to her, it is plain, was if not a clear conscience then at least a lessened sense of personal guilt. By abstaining from political involvement, she wrote, one still adopts a position. 'It is not possible to fix a day, a week, or even a month for the conversion that then worked within me. But it is indubitable that the spring of 1939 marks a break in my life. I renounced my individualism, my anti-humanism. I learned solidarity', she wrote in *La Force de l'âge*.[10]

What precisely did this 'conversion' of hers entail? In her autobiography she repeatedly accuses herself of self-deception in the 1930s: her ostrich-like behaviour in refusing to recognise that war was inevitable; her disinclination to face facts — 'my blindness, my ignorance'; the way she clung to the hope that she could somehow avoid the kind of tragedy that was overwhelming the lives of so many of her contemporaries in the rest of Europe. This self-deception is seen as a shocking mistake or worse by the Simone de Beauvoir of 1959–60, as she looks back over the attitude of her earlier self, aged thirty at the time of Munich. Here was a woman of left-wing sympathies who had struggled against following where those sympathies should, in theory, have led her — to the side of the committed left-wing radicals or Communists. Yet actually this 'conversion' of 1939 produced no such immediate effect. The new 'solidarity' was still a notion, an awareness of the legitimate claims of other people, a form of sympathy, rather than an active variety of political commitment.

It is curious that the date given for her 'conversion', spring 1939, some months before the outbreak of war (in September), apparently antedates that of Sartre, although he is often depicted in her memoirs as showing a greater sense of realism during the long period of self-styled self-deception. According to her autobiography, Sartre himself (who had been mobilised) did not formulate a new morality until he came home on leave in February 1940. This new morality, based on the idea of authenticity, required each man to take responsibility for his situation (*assumer sa situation*). The sole means of doing this, Sartre believed, was to transcend that situation by committing oneself to some form of action. Any other attitude was futile and rooted in bad faith (*mauvaise foi*). By early 1940, then, Sartre — in theory at least — had gone further along the road to political commitment than she had; but she proclaimed in *La Force de l'âge* that she had at once accepted his new attitude as her own. That remains to be seen.

The swift German advance of May 1940, the hasty exodus from Paris in which she joined, the defeat of the French in June (Sartre was taken prisoner, his friend Paul Nizan had been killed in May, Jacques-Laurent Bost was wounded) left Simone de Beauvoir in a state close to despair. The Germans made their triumphal entry into the stunned capital, and divided the country into two zones: the northern section under their own occupation, the southern section or so-called 'free zone' under their client regime at Vichy.

On 28 June 1940, Simone de Beauvoir returned to occupied Paris, and to teaching philosophy. Soon, a serious step was demanded of her. In order to continue at her teaching post, she signed a declaration that she was neither a Freemason nor a Jew. She states that she found it repugnant to do this, adding that nobody refused to sign. The fact was that people could only go on working with the express permission of the Germans and on the conditions laid down by them. In this way, everyone who had to work to eat was compromised. As Simone de Beauvoir herself puts it — and she is one of the supreme witnesses and recorders of this terrible and equivocal period — 'the very fact of breathing implied a compromise'.[11]

The atmosphere in the capital was dreary: there were no private cars to be seen because there was no petrol; people went about on bicycles. Food was in short supply despite the rationing system. That extremely cold winter of 1940–1, because her room was unheated, she wrote the last chapters of her novel *L'Invitée* and revised it in Le Dôme, where some warmth could be found. From Vichy there came the stream of what Richard Cobb has called 'the snivelling vocabulary of cloying hypocrisy and sack-cloth and ashes *mea culpa, mea culpa*, retribution and atonement, poured out nasally from Radio Vichy, as if the station had been taken over by battalions of French Uriah Heeps . . .'.[12] The Vichy regime's anti-Jewish measures were inaugurated, its instruments often eager to prove themselves more zealous than their German masters.

In Paris, the Fascist writer Pierre Drieu La Rochelle had taken charge of the leading literary journal, *La Nouvelle Revue Française*. From the weekly, *Je suis partout*, there issued the denunciations of individuals that were penned by another Fascist writer, Robert Brasillach, denunciations which could prove literally fatal to the victims. No book could be published, no play could be staged, without the sanction of the German authorities. Consequently, all those who remained in the occupied zone and who went about their profession must be compromised, in Simone de Beauvoir's view. Perhaps, ideally, the companions could have gone abroad into exile before the débâcle, like a number of their contemporaries, but Sartre certainly did not wish to elude any experience that befell his country.

Eventually, Sartre was released from Stalag XII D in March 1941. At thirty-six, he returned a changed character, deeply affected by his contact with men from all walks of life both in the army and in the prisoner of war camp. She was surprised by his stern moral attitude. He strongly disapproved of the fact that she bought tea on the black market, and roundly declared that she was wrong to have signed the declaration that she was neither a Freemason nor a Jew. Somehow, it had been simpler for the anti-Fascists in the prison camp to refuse to compromise: but how was she to continue as a teacher without doing so?

Besides, Sartre was now seriously determined to commit himself to action. In her account, she declares that she was completely stunned by this development (although, as we have seen, in the memoirs she attributed his desire for action to an earlier period: February 1940). She argued with him, stressing their isolation, their impotence; and she remained sceptical about his urge to organise some sort of resistance to the Germans. Thus the statement of her own 'conversion' to solidarity, attributed to the spring of 1939, seems premature, not only in the light of her conduct in signing the declaration of her 'Aryan' credentials, but also in view of her own critical attitude to his new desire to become involved in opposition to the occupying power.

Sartre himself resumed his teaching post at the Lycée Pasteur (which he had obtained in 1937), presumably on the same terms as his companion; and he began to make contact with like-minded anti-Nazi individuals and groups. Their own movement, to be called 'Socialism and Liberty', thus embodying 'their' programme (or rather, Sartre's), was to concern itself with the gathering of information to be spread by the printed word. He had decided that they should spend their holidays in the summer of 1941 in the unoccupied zone, so as to try to enlist the aid of various notabilities who were residing there.

The companions made their slow way by bicycle to Marseilles, where Sartre had an unsatisfactory meeting with the Socialist politician, Daniel Mayer. Then, in the vicinity of Grasse, Sartre found André Gide equally elusive. In Malraux's villa at Saint-Jean-Cap-Ferrat, the would-be *résistant* was stylishly received by the author of *La Condition humaine*, who told him that action seemed for the present to be inopportune. And that was the end of 'Socialism and Liberty' — 'our movement' as she calls it. (Sartre tried to make contact with the Communists, but was rebuffed.) It seems quite clear from her account, however, that she herself was not present at any of Sartre's abortive interviews with leading figures. Only later in *La Force de l'âge* does she speak of her enthusiasm for 'Socialism and Liberty' because of its 'risky improvisation', contradicting her own earlier scepticism about the enterprise.[13]

The companions turned back from the idea of action to literature. She began work on a novel treating the subject of resistance to the Germans, to be called *Le Sang des autres*, which she knew could not be published until after the War. It was, she said, inspired by Sartre's realisation of the risks that he would have made his friends incur if he had not abandoned 'Socialism and Liberty'. To be responsible for the death of somebody else by persisting with the 'movement' — that would scarcely be forgivable, they agreed. Already, among other groups, some friends of theirs, including one of her star pupils, had been deported to Germany (and were never to return). As she makes her *alter ego*, Anne, say in the postwar novel, *Les Mandarins*: 'It was not to me that the real misfortunes had happened yet they had haunted my life . . .'.[14] In that sorrow, perhaps, there lay the roots of a change of heart.

Controversy still rages over conduct in France from 1940–4, and over the degree to which individuals were compromised by collaboration with the Germans. Simone de Beauvoir refers to those years in her memoirs as 'a period so equivocal that the very memory I have of it is blurred. I really often felt, after peace returned, how difficult it was to speak of it to someone who did not live through it . . .'.[15] It is only natural, perhaps, that those who did live through it should try to put the best interpretation on their actions. Attitudes to that age may be divided into those which try to take a detached historical view, and those which express a stern moral judgement.

On the one hand, for the English historian Richard Cobb: 'what was a waiter to do except wait . . .? *Occupants* and *occupés* at least agreed that life had to go on: an eminently sensible aim'.[16] That is surely to take a baser view of human behaviour than did many of those humble people who risked their lives; nor is it one with which Simone de Beauvoir herself would have concurred. Somewhat less cynical though eminently realistic is the view of the American cultural historian and biographer, Herbert R. Lottman, who calmly heads Chapter 19 of his study, *The Left Bank*, 'Everybody Collaborated'.

On the other hand, there are those whose stance is one of severity and high patriotism. Among these is the English novelist, David Pryce-Jones in his book, *Paris in the Third Reich*. Another is the American biographer, Phyllis Grosskurth, who asks accusingly of Sartre and Simone de Beauvoir: '. . . what about their reactions to what was being done to the Jews in their midst?'[17] As regards the responses of the author of *Le Sang des autres*, however, there is plenty of evidence about her sense of impotent horror at the fate of the Jews. The philosopher, Vladimir Jankélévitch, attributed Sartre's pro-Communist commitment after the Liberation to his remorse at his lack of courage during the Occupation, since at that time he had continued writing and pursuing his career as a teacher without a single act of protest against the dismissal of his Jewish colleagues.[18] The same reproach could have been levelled at Simone de Beauvoir. Be that as it may, the reproof shows little sense of the limitations of the day: such an act of protest would have been otiose and would have led to their own removal or worse. One did not protest against the Nazis, one went underground.

The fact remains, however, that both Sartre and Simone de Beauvoir won fame during the German Occupation. His play, *Les Mouches*, performed by Charles Dullin's company at the Théâtre de la Cité (hitherto known as the Théâtre Sarah-Bernhardt after the great French Jewish actress), did not at the time have quite the political resonance that Simone de Beauvoir suggests in her memoirs. As for her novel, *L'Invitée*, it was published in 1943 to great acclaim, being welcomed not only in the clandestine press but by journals which collaborated with the occupying power. She was touched when Ramon Fernandez, who never came to the café de Flore and who figured among known collaborators, called there especially to congratulate her.

As it happens, there is little that is political about *L'Invitée* except the date of its publication. Nor, significantly, is there anything relating to solidarity. The murder of Xavière with which it ends is presented as an act of deliberate individual choice: 'Finally, she had chosen. She had chosen herself', are the last words of the book, which refer to Françoise's deed.[19] Simone de Beauvoir had high hopes of winning the Goncourt prize with this novel, and would have been delighted to receive it, although the judges of the Académie Goncourt were known to include collaborators among their number. According to Herbert Lottman, these writers had already been warned by the Communist front organisation, the Comité National des Ecrivains, that they would have much to answer for after the Liberation.[20] Sartre informed her that the CNE would allow her to accept the prize, provided that she gave no interviews or articles to the press. However, her hopes were dashed.

Meanwhile, in 1943, Simone de Beauvoir was summarily dismissed from her teaching position. The mother of her pupil, Nathalie Sorokine (called 'Lise' in the autobiography), had accused Simone de Beauvoir of leading the girl astray. Instead of making a 'good marriage', Nathalie chose to live with a budding poet, a Jewish pupil of Sartre's, young Jean-Pierre Bourla. (He figures as the much lamented Diégo in *Les Mandarins*.) This dismissal meant that Simone de Beauvoir could not teach anywhere else either.

As a result, she began to work as a producer for Radio Vichy, whose propaganda was so largely concerned with the Pétainist themes she hated: family and nationhood, self-abasement and atonement. According to her, writers who were opposed to the Germans (unnamed — Sartre and herself?) had decided that they would not contribute to papers and magazines in the occupied zone, or give talks on Radio Paris; but they allowed themselves to write for journals in the unoccupied sector and to speak on Radio Vichy provided the content was innocuous. Her own programme, she relates, concerned ancient festivals from the Middle Ages onwards. In her autobiography, she emphasises that such work for Vichy's propaganda machine was permitted by her left-wing associates; and perhaps the lady appears to protest too much. It was certainly a less heroic task than that undertaken by her characters, the clandestine Resistance fighters of *Le Sang des autres*.

In that novel, which possibly helped to endow its author with Resistance credentials, the apolitical Hélène finally joins the Resistance after witnessing a round-up of Jews for deportation to Germany. To Hélène's horror, a mother is separated from her small daughter, Ruth; the woman runs after her, crying her name as the policeman puts the weeping little girl on the bus with the other Jewish children. Hélène asks herself: 'Is there nothing we can do? Supposing together we all fell on the policeman? Supposing we tore the child from him? But nobody moved'. The bystanders, like Hélène, are rooted to the spot. '"Oh! Why? Why?" thought Hélène despairingly. She wept, but she remained motionless like the others, and looked on . . . "I watched History passing by! It was my history. All this is happening to me."' The dying Hélène, wounded in action, cries out 'Ruth! Ruth!' to the mystification of her hearers.[21]

Ultimately, though, it is less the fate of French Jews as a whole than the fate of Jewish acquaintances of hers in the Resistance who had been captured and executed, or of friends who disappeared forever into the death camps, that gave Simone de Beauvoir an overpowering feeling of guilt and completed her conversion to a sense of responsibility. She felt profound sorrow at the betrayal and death of the young Jewish poet, Jean-Pierre Bourla, of whom she was especially fond. 'Each morning, as I opened my eyes, I stole the world from him', she cried in *La Force de l'âge*. With the death of Bourla, she wrote: '. . . never had I touched so nearly the capricious horror of our mortal condition'.[22] And this conversion occurred much nearer to 1943–4 than to 1939.

As she was to say long afterwards, in 1974, in an interview with Caroline Moorehead: 'My real encounter with the world and politics was the War. . . . I realised I had led a very sheltered life.

I lived the War with the feeling that I was a pawn of political forces . . .'.[23] (Sartre said much the same.) The conversion of which she speaks so eloquently in *La Force de l'âge* is the commitment of a now famous writer to protest against injustice in the years after the War, when it was not only possible but, under a restored democracy, with rare exceptions, safe to do so.

Notes

1. *La Force de l'âge*, p. 34.
2. Ibid., p. 140.
3. Ibid., pp. 296–7.
4. Sartre, *Situations* X, p. 178.
5. *La Force de l'âge*, p. 152.
6. Ibid., p. 172.
7. Ibid., pp. 224, 272–3; Sartre, *Situations* X, p. 178.
8. Sarah Hirschman, quoted in C. Francis and F. Gontier, *Les Ecrits de Simone de Beauvoir*, p. 22; see also their *Simone de Beauvoir*, pp. 167–8.
9. *La Force de l'âge*, p. 345.
10. Ibid., p. 368.
11. Ibid., p. 493.
12. Richard Cobb, *French and Germans, Germans and French*, University Press of New England, 1983, p. 133.
13. *La Force de l'âge*, p. 550.
14. Ibid., p. 513, note 1.
15. Ibid., p. 513.
16. Richard Cobb, *French and Germans*, pp. 62–4.
17. Phyllis Grosskurth, review of Anne Whitmarsh, *Simone de Beauvoir and the Limits of Commitment*, *The Times Literary Supplement*, 25 August 1981.
18. Béatrice Berlowitz, 'Le Débat autour de Vladimir Jankélévitch'; and Michel Contat, 'Les Philosophes sous l'Occupation', *Le Monde*, 28 June 1985.
19. *L'Invitée*, p. 441.
20. Herbert R. Lottman, *The Left Bank*, Heinemann, 1982, p. 168.
21. *Le Sang des autres*, Gallimard, 1945, pp. 204, 212–15.
22. *La Force de l'âge*, pp. 592–3.
23. Interview with Caroline Moorehead (2), *The Times*, 16 May 1974.

5 Politics: The Years of Fame

For Simone de Beauvoir, as for Sartre, the immense international literary fame that they suddenly attained in 1944 as 'Resistant intellectuals' was to be used to demonstrate their passsionate involvement in political issues; their refusal to be 'accomplices' of what they considered to be evil policies; and, above all, the essential rightness of their position and their feelings. The stands they were to adopt throughout the rest of their lives derived in large part from the aura and prestige of the Resistance and, to some degree, from their own unease and bad conscience.

The myth of an unremitting intellectual resistance to the Nazis, which supposedly functioned heroically throughout the German Occupation, took hold at the Liberation. Of course, there were writers who were actively engaged in the underground struggle for years, but they were mostly not the ones who stood out in the limelight in 1945.

The myth was fostered abroad — doubtless innocently — by such London-based organs as the influential Francophile magazine, *Horizon*. Nancy Cunard, one-time mistress of the Communist poet, Louis Aragon, wrote there in her 'Letter from Paris' (published in June 1945) that Resistance writers and poets were grouped in the Comité National des Ecrivains, thanks mainly to him. She spoke of Sartre, who was to be seen writing at the café de Flore, adding: 'there is almost a "School of the Café de Flore" — that of the most active of the numerous resistance groups'.[1] For Cyril Connolly, the editor of *Horizon*, after a visit to Paris, 'the literature of occupation' (apart from writers who collaborated with the Germans) spelt notably Jean-Paul Sartre and the Algerian-born author of *L'Etranger*, Albert Camus. Moreover, 'nearly all the "occupation" writers were also in the resistance movement', Connolly asserted.[2]

In his view, Sartre occupied 'a dominating position in the world of French literature today' with the stress on political commitment, 'an attitude to literature which is held by the Resistant intellectuals'.[3] If the new stars were Sartre and Camus, Simone de Beauvoir was seen to be revolving in their orbit. Part of their attraction was that they fitted, or rather were made to fit into, the noble role of unswervingly active *résistants* in the intellectual and literary field. Simone de Beauvoir herself contributed to the myth when she wrote in an article entitled 'Jean-Paul Sartre. Strictly Personal' for the American magazine *Harper's Bazaar* (January 1946) that the philosopher played 'an active part in the Resistance'.[4]

The picture, as we have seen, was neither so simple nor so heroic. The companions had early dismantled their resistance group, 'Socialism and Liberty', set up in 1941 mainly to disseminate information: this effort became too risky and was short-lived. Simone de Beauvoir had not warmed to it at the time. It is true that by 1942 a collaborator like the novelist Drieu La Rochelle, Sartre's *bête noire*, could see that the Germans were not going to win the War. Yet it was not until 1943 that Sartre began to attend clandestine meetings of the Communist-dominated Comité National des Ecrivains. His companion did not join him there because of what she later termed 'a scruple'.

She enlarged upon this 'scruple' as follows: 'My agreement with Sartre was so whole-hearted', she wrote in *La Force de l'âge*, 'that my attendance would quite pointlessly have seconded his: it seemed to me that as it was futile it became ill-timed and flashy. . . . I should have liked "to do something"; but I shrank from symbolic involvement and I stayed at home'.[5] This curious explanation on the grounds of 'personal embarrassment' and reliance on Sartre's commitment as the expression of her own, seems strange in a woman who avowedly valued her independence so highly. The fact that Sartre found the CNE sessions 'tedious' was scarcely sufficient reason for her to stay away from them. The episode gives some idea of her dependence on Sartre at the time, and of their relationship where the subject of political commitment was concerned.

However, it was in the latter half of 1943 that, following upon his own recent involvement, Albert Camus recruited both Sartre and Simone de Beauvoir, under the pseudonyms of Miro and Castor, for *Combat*. (This was a resistance movement since 1942, before the name was employed for an underground newspaper.) Curiously, in her autobiography, she ascribes the connection to Sartre alone. She had just met Camus at the café de Flore (though Sartre had already made his acquaintance at the public dress-rehearsal of *Les Mouches*). In the months that followed, Camus was often to be found with the companions and their court. He was fun to be with, even if he was fond of telling risqué jokes at which she affected to be shocked; and he joined in the 'fiestas' or parties where writers and artists danced or played the fool and consumed a great deal of alcohol. According to his biographer, Herbert Lottman, Camus did not share in the work of *Combat* as a resistance group, but served only in the production of its clandestine newspaper from the end of 1943. And it was for the newspaper that he had recruited the companions.

In the summer of 1944, with the arrest of Jacqueline Bernard by the Gestapo — she was the editorial secretary of *Combat* and the link between members of the team — the companions, duly warned by Camus, sought refuge in the home of the Surrealist writer, Michel Leiris. Then they moved to an inn in the country, where they went walking and continued writing. They did not return to Paris until August 1944, after learning that the American armies were nearing Chartres. Neither of them wished to miss the liberation of Paris.

The period that ensued was one of intense euphoria. Simone de Beauvoir wrote not long afterwards, in her 'Pour une Morale de l'ambiguïté': 'The moments that followed the liberation of Paris . . . were a huge collective festival. . . . All those who had made this struggle their own, if only by the sincerity of their hopes, considered this victory as absolute, whatever the future might bring'.[6] The words, 'if only by the sincerity of their hopes', perhaps give an accurate reflection of her true position during the time of trial: that of someone whose heart was in the right place on the side of the Allies. Later in the same work, though, she declared that 'all the French anti-Fascists were united during the Occupation by their common resistance against the oppressor'.[7] If this includes Sartre and herself, it implies a more active, positive and long-standing involvement in the Resistance movement than they can legitimately claim.

That they, with Camus, were latecomers to active participation was by no means out of the ordinary. In fact, their role consisted of journalism (and in Sartre's case, of literary politics in the CNE, which drew up blacklists of collaborationist writers whom its members pursued at the time of the Liberation). Even André Malraux, who led the Alsace-Lorraine brigade to victory, did not commit himself to active military resistance on behalf of General de Gaulle until the beginning of 1944. If, in the exultation of triumph, outsiders wished to grant the companions a fuller and more heroic part than they actually played, it was hardly for them to issue disclaimers and denials at such a moment — or even later. (And perhaps in the course of time they came to believe that they had done and risked more than they had in actuality. Certainly, Simone de Beauvoir gives to Robert Dubreuilh, the figure loosely based on Sartre in *Les Mandarins*, an active and committed role in the prewar anti-Fascist movement as well as in the Resistance. Readers who mistakenly assumed that Dubreuilh was a carbon copy of Sartre could be misled.)

It was only many years afterwards that the conduct of the companions began to be probed more rigorously and dispassionately. Now it can be seen that in her autobiography Simone de Beauvoir antedates the moment of her 'conversion' for a good reason. This move serves as a kind of strategy to convey the impression that her political involvement was of longer duration and greater consistency than it had been in reality.

Interestingly, whatever their hopes of Allied victory, at no time were the companions in favour of General de Gaulle, leader of military resistance from the Fall of France in 1940. They remained suspicious of his right-wing background and of his intentions, always seeing in him the shadow of the dictator.

The Liberation was marked by a settling of scores. Women who had become too friendly with the Nazi soldiery were humiliated by having their heads shaved in public. People suspected of collaboration with the occupying power were summarily shot. It is now believed that over ten thousand were executed in this way: not all of them were guilty. This was the period known as *l'épuration* (the great purge). As so often happens at such moments, the smaller fry are caught in the net while the big fish contrive to escape. However, one writer of talent, who had been in the forefront of the literary collaborators, was put on trial in January 1945. This was the novelist and literary critic, Robert Brasillach, whom Simone de Beauvoir particularly detested for his denunciations of individuals in *Je suis partout*. For her, he stood out as one of those who had helped to cause the death of her friends.

She attended the trial, where she felt distinctly uneasy, for she was at once struck by Brasillach's courageous and dignified bearing, which could not but inspire respect. Everything suddenly seemed oddly ambiguous. The ritual of justice — with the magistrates engaged in their customary task, the detached journalists, the public present out of mere curiosity — disturbed her by its abstract nature. In any case, following the Surrealists, she often tended to sympathise with the accused person as a victim of society. 'Punishment assumes then the aspect of a symbolic demonstration and the condemned man is close to appearing as an expiatory victim. . .',[8] she wrote in the essay 'Œil pour œil' ('An Eye for an Eye'). With Brasillach, there was a kind of dissociation between the accused and his crimes because of the time that had elapsed before his trial, so that he looked different from the person who had committed them. In this sense, all punishment seemed a failure.

Momentarily inclined to heed the voice of Christian charity, she resisted it. 'We can make excuses for every offence and even every crime by means of which individuals assert themselves against society', she noted speciously, while adding more tellingly: 'but when a man deliberately sets out to degrade a human being into a thing, he provokes a scandal for which there can be no amends. That is the sole sin against man: when it occurs no indulgence is permissible and it is for man to punish it'. To degrade a human creature into a thing is a form of absolute evil and it calls for vengeance, she wrote. Christians may opt for charity, but in her view those who do not share Christian belief must follow human morality. Because Brasillach did not repudiate his past — on the contrary, by his courageous stand he affirmed his solidarity with it and responsibility for it — he had to be punished. Whatever element of failure remained in such punishment, whatever the sense of ambiguity, nevertheless 'to punish is to recognise that man is free in evil as in good . . .'.[9] In 'Œil pour œil' she plainly reveals her disquiet and her need to justify her stand in resisting the Christian argument.

She refused to sign the petition to save Brasillach's life, a petition keenly supported by the Catholic novelist, François Mauriac. Camus, who at first had agreed with Simone de Beauvoir, changed his mind and added his signature, largely because he was opposed to the death penalty. This was one of the things she

61

came to hold against him. In any case, General de Gaulle declined to pardon Brasillach, who faced a firing squad on 6 February 1945, the only French literary collaborator to be executed.

Years afterwards, in *La Force des choses*, Simone de Beauvoir did not waver: 'I have never felt any regrets about not signing', she wrote. She knew that words can kill: 'There are words as murderous as a gas chamber'. And she went on: 'In the case of Brasillach . . . by his denunciations, by his calls for assassination and genocide, he had directly collaborated with the Gestapo'.[10] Yet, in the light of the Algerian War, she now felt that in her essay 'Œil pour œil' she had justified *l'épuration* without adducing the one really solid argument: that killers and torturers should be executed not in order to prove that man is free to choose good or evil but as a deterrent. In those days, she now felt, she had been insufficiently liberated from the ideology of her class. So her justification of *l'épuration* had grown firmer with time. Today, Brasillach (however guilty) may appear as the scapegoat when other writers like Céline and Rebatet, who were equally compromised, escaped the net to bask in literary adulation. Would a less uncompromising attitude on her part have repudiated her Resistance credentials?

Meanwhile, the world that had long looked to France for the latest intellectual fashion, now found what it sought in the French version of existentialism — the companions, along with Camus, being chosen as the supreme votaries of a new cult. The newspapers, of course, were not interested in literary divergences and philosophical niceties. It was not just the writings of Sartre, Beauvoir and Camus, but the whole ambience of Saint-Germain-des-Prés that provided copy: the cafés and bars that they frequented, the night-clubs and jazz clubs where they were to be seen, like the cellar of Le Tabou made famous by the writer and jazz trumpeter, Boris Vian. The singer (and later film actress) Juliette Gréco, with her pale face and straight dark hair, a figure clothed in unadorned black from head to foot, symbolised French existentialism for the uninitiated: something sad and pessimistic, yet fascinatingly novel, 'postwar', and *à la mode*.

At first, the companions objected to the label 'existentialist' and then they decided to accept it. There was much public controversy: Catholics as well as Marxists attacked existentialism. The new magazine, *Les Temps Modernes*, which Sartre and Simone de Beauvoir founded in association with Raymond Aron, Merleau-Ponty, Michel Leiris and others, engaged in ideological disputes, at first with opponents. Then the members of the editorial board began to differ among themselves, some (including Raymond Aron and Merleau-Ponty) soon took their departure.

All this disputation simply added to public interest, and to the notoriety of 'la grande Sartreuse' or 'Notre-Dame de Sartre', as the wits liked to call her. (The papers printed lurid accounts of her supposedly outrageous and immoral goings-on.) She was writing philosophical and polemical essays, and giving lectures in Paris and abroad (in Spain and Portugal, Tunisia and Algeria, Italy and Switzerland). In addition, she was publishing her novels, *Le Sang des autres* and *Tous les Hommes sont mortels*, though her only play, *Les Bouches inutiles*, folded after some fifty performances at the Théâtre des Carrefours. A few years later, the publication of *Le Deuxième sexe* would make her one of the most famous and controversial women writers in the world.

With the Liberation, celebrated and admired authors arrived in Paris. Not least among these was Ernest Hemingway. The companions visited the author of *For Whom the Bell Tolls* in his room at the Ritz, staying until the small hours and imbibing a good deal of whisky. They enjoyed a more sustained relationship for a time with the Hungarian-born novelist, Arthur Koestler, for whose memoir, *Spanish Testament* — with its account of his prison experiences during the Spanish Civil War when he was condemned to death — Sartre had expressed admiration years before. Koestler's wife, Mamaine, recalled leaving her husband (very drunk) with Simone de Beauvoir in the bar du Pont-Royal. On another occasion, the Koestlers went out to dinner with the companions and Camus and his wife. Afterwards, they went to a dance-hall, and from thence to a Russian night-club, where musicians played soulful gypsy music. According to Mamaine, Sartre and Koestler became drunk, Simone de Beauvoir 'wept a great deal', huge quantities of vodka and champagne having been consumed.[11] Then the party ajourned to a bistro for onion soup, oysters and white wine. Small wonder that combativeness sometimes replaced conviviality.

It was not long before quarrels arose between Sartre and Koestler. One concerned a contributor to the influential radical New York magazine, *Partisan Review*. Koestler defended him, challenging Sartre's right to speak of liberty when he edited a journal like *Les Temps Modernes* which followed the Communist Party line and thus 'condoned' the deportation of millions of human beings from the Baltic States, as well as other crimes. Having sobered up, Koestler sent an apology which Sartre accepted. A few months later, Simone de Beauvoir was annoyed when Koestler failed to defend Sartre in a bar in her presence. The fact was that Koestler treated as obvious nonsense the suggestion, made by a Gaullist who was drunk, that Sartre had offered his services to General de Gaulle, whereas Simone de Beauvoir took the whole incident seriously.

The following year, relations between the companions and Koestler were broken off: no friend of André Malraux's could be a friend of theirs, after the now Gaullist author of *La Condition humaine* had used his influence to try to prevent the publication of *Les Temps Modernes*. According to Mamaine Koestler: 'Simone made a great speech to K in which she said how awful the Americans were and how Russia was really the country of the great proletarian revolution . . .'.[12] And this harangue was addressed to the ex-Communist author of *Darkness at Noon*, who had himself served the Communist propaganda machine before the War, who knew its workings from the inside, and who had seen his friends disappear one by one in Stalin's dread purges.

That there was more to this quarrel than purely ideological matters now seems likely. According to Simone de Beauvoir's joint biographers, Claude Francis and Fernande Gontier, she was 'briefly' attracted to the womanising Koestler.[13] In *Les Mandarins*, she would depict him as the obsessive anti-Stalinist, Victor Scriassine, with some distaste. Koestler regarded her portrait of himself in her memoirs as 'a rather vitriolic caricature'. In his view, her portrayal of his encounter with Camus and the companions offered 'a sadly distorted echo'. He added, though, that there were private reasons for her hostility 'which are too trivial to go into . . .', while accusing himself of being a 'male chauvinist', unable to take seriously any female intellectual who ventured to write on political philosophy.[14] Certainly, in *Les Mandarins*, the author's *alter ego*, Anne, senses that Scriassine does not take her at her true worth; he also reveals his hostility to all women intellectuals. Their embraces in Scriassine's room at the Ritz (shades of the companions' visit to Hemingway!) prove to be a depressing fiasco.

For his part, Koestler accused Simone de Beauvoir of possessiveness and domination where Sartre was concerned. He described a chance meeting with Sartre on a train (in 1950) when their friendship was very briefly renewed. If 'la Simone' had been with Sartre, Koestler did not think that this easy intercourse would have been possible. In his memoirs Raymond Aron was to remark how his own close friendship with Sartre at the Ecole Normale Supérieure came to an end when Simone de Beauvoir entered the scene. This 'domination', however, had its limits.

With the end of the War, French intellectuals could again travel abroad: in turn, both Sartre and Camus had been invited to lecture in the United States. During a visit to New York, Sartre had met Dolorès Vanetti (known as 'M' in Simone de Beauvoir's autobiography), one-time actress and mistress of the writer André Breton, leader of the Surrealist movement. (Breton had spent the War in the United States — exile being one way of emerging from the conflict with unsullied reputation.) With Dolorès Vanetti, now married to an American, Sartre had encountered one of the 'serious' amorous episodes of his life, and he proposed to spend several months of each year with her.

All this could scarcely be music to Simone de Beauvoir's ears. She wondered whether Sartre cared more for Dolorès than for herself. At last she could contain herself no longer, and one day she risked asking him whether this was indeed the case. 'I am extremely attached to [Dolorès], but it's you I'm with', he replied.[15] She understood this to mean that he was adhering to their pact, and nothing more. The whole future seemed to her to be at risk.

She herself had been invited to lecture in the United States, and she set off on 27 January 1947 to examine the problems of the postwar writer, as well as the role of women in contemporary society, on university campuses across the country. The visit was to last four months, and the prospect filled her with excitement and exhilaration. Had she not been stimulated by American novels, films and jazz? She was going to encounter a veritable myth. Had she not welcomed American soldiers at the Liberation as the embodiment of freedom not only for the French but even for the world as a whole? True, this enthusiasm was short-lived. As for Sartre, he had not warmed to the United States, and he doubtless conveyed his jaundiced views to his companion. He had met Richard Wright, the author of *Black Boy*, who at that time was still a member of the Communist Party. It was Richard Wright who would take her around Harlem and show her something of the grim problems facing the American Blacks. To him and to his wife Ellen she dedicated her book, *L'Amérique au jour le jour* — though she was to break with him after he left the Party to join with Koestler and all those for whom the god had failed.

Unlike Sartre, Simone de Beauvoir could speak English, if with a strong accent. She doubtless felt that she understood more than she actually did. Accustomed to draw rapid conclusions from her immediate impressions and encounters, she had complete confidence in the perfect rightness of her judgment. And she would draw conclusions about a vast country, its varied population, its complex history and intricate political traditions, on the strength of small samples, not always accurately perceived (a process she would follow in her travels to other lands).

From reading the newspapers she deduced that the very semblance of democracy was fading in the United States, and that arbitrary government was gaining ground (this was before the advent of the witch hunt led by Senator Joseph McCarthy from 1950). Discussions with the staff of *Partisan Review*, by then a deeply anti-Stalinist journal, made her decide that all American intellectuals were lacking in nuance and subtlety. New York intellectuals (along with American university students) did not discuss political and social questions, she opined: 'I know, of course, that there is no political life in America . . .'.[16] American intellectuals were conformist, chauvinistic, neurotically anti-Communist (and besides, there was no way of shaking their convictions!). As for American women, they remained in a state of utter dependence — a view that she had not changed by the early 1960s. She (who scorned the workings of the parliamentary system) could speak of the pretence of American democracy. In America, the individual is nothing, she declared, although he is the object of an abstract cult. While acknowledging the generosity of people she encountered, she regretted that she could not feel more warmly towards the country as a whole.

It is scarcely surprising that *L'Amérique au jour le jour* raised hackles in the United States. The novelist, Mary McCarthy, penned a telling essay entitled 'Mlle Gulliver en Amérique', which sharply and wittily commented on the book's distortions, on the consistent misspelling of famous names (an irritating habit continued in the autobiography and other writings). 'What is more pathetic is her credulity, which amounts to a kind of superstition. She is so eager to appear well-informed that she believes anything anybody tells her, especially if it is anti-American and pretends to reveal the inner workings of the capitalist mechanism', wrote Mary McCarthy with pained indignation.[17]

L'Amérique au jour le jour, published in 1948, takes the form of a diary, but it was put together afterwards with the help of notes, correspondence and recollections. None the less, Simone de Beauvoir maintained that it was perfectly true to her spontaneous impressions of the moment. This cannot be entirely so, for her total view must have coloured her first impressions. And her total view was undoubtedly affected by her contact with the left-wing novelist, Nelson Algren, in what she was to depict as the most passionate affair of her life.

Passing through Chicago in February 1947, armed with an introduction, she telephoned Algren who, because of her accent, failed to comprehend her and rang off. She tried again several times, and finally, without much enthusiasm, he agreed to meet this persistent Frenchwoman at her hotel. The importance of this encounter with a disaffected American radical for the development and consolidation of Simone de Beauvoir's later political attitudes should not be underestimated.

Born in Detroit, of Swedish and German Jewish descent, Nelson Algren was then a year younger than his visitor, and a man of rugged good looks. He was brought up in poverty in Chicago, and throughout his life he remained the poetic chronicler of the down-and-outs, drug-addicts, petty criminals and prostitutes whom he met on the road and with whom he associated in the Polish district of the city where he continued to live. During the dark years of the Depression he had been a migratory worker: he had travelled the freight trains, and had even spent time in jail in Texas for the theft of a typewriter. Like so many others, he was shattered and permanently scarred by his experiences during that period of hardship and disillusion. Algren belonged with the American tradition of writing about personal experiences of low life whose leading exponents included Jack London and John Dos Passos, a tradition still flourishing in the work of William Kennedy. When he met Simone de Beauvoir, Algren was already well known for his novel *Never Come Morning* (1942), but he had not yet published the two books that were to establish his reputation as a member of the distinct Chicago school.

As for the author of *L'Invitée*, approaching forty, she was ready for an adventure, deeply shaken as she was by the degree of Sartre's attachment to Dolorès Vanetti. In September 1947 she returned to Chicago for two weeks, having broken off the second-ary or 'contingent' liaison with Jacques-Laurent Bost. Nelson Algren took her around *his* Chicago — she had always made a point of visiting with Sartre the more disreputable areas of foreign cities, and now, in the story-teller of *The Neon Wilderness* she had found the perfect guide. In his company she visited the doss-houses and the sleazy bars with their denizens whom he knew so well. She was shocked by such extreme squalor in a land of enormous wealth and power. Through Algren, she would meet tramps and beggars; see the electric chair in the County prison; and tour the stockyards so memorably depicted by Upton Sinclair in *The Jungle*.

The tenor of Algren's remarks about his native land may be deduced from a passage about the lost souls of the lower depths in his novel, *The Man with the Golden Arm*: 'The great, secret and special American guilt of owning nothing, nothing at all, in the one land where ownership and virtue are one. . . . All had gone stale for these disinherited. . . . On Skid Row even the native-born no longer felt they had been born in America'.[18] Such an attitude of alienation *vis-à-vis* their country was common enough among intellectuals who had experienced the Great Depression at first hand. Like so many of his contemporaries, Nelson Algren became a Communist, though he was one no longer when Simone de Beauvoir met him. He was among those oversimplifiers who were convinced of the decay of capitalism, and whose sympathies lay with the cause of revolution. It is plain, then, that intellectually

Nelson Algren and Simone de Beauvoir had much in common. What he did was to show her the worst and darkest side of American life, confirm her prejudices, and inculcate an extreme view of the country as one of exploiters and exploited, a view from which she would never depart, and which would harden with the years.

Her meeting with Algren and her slumming with him are depicted in *L'Amérique au jour le jour*, where he figures as 'N.A.'. Details of their passionate affair were later to be revealed in *Les Mandarins*, dedicated to the American writer, so that the identity of the model for Anne's lover, Lewis Brogan, in that novel, becomes immediately obvious to the most cursory reader. The fictional pair repeat the journey made in 1948 by Nelson Algren and Simone de Beauvoir, by Mississipi steamboat to New Orleans, calling at *ante-bellum* mansions along the way. From thence they travelled to Mexico and Guatemala. Algren proposed marriage. She declined: even without the pact with Sartre, she knew perfectly well that she could not have functioned as a writer outside France. Nor could Algren, a writer rooted in Chicago, consider exile in Paris. They were both torn, and he particularly resented her stance, as she was to tell in *La Force des choses*.

On her return to Paris, an unpleasant surprise awaited her. She was expecting to go on the usual holiday with Sartre, but he had yielded to the complaints of Dolorès Vanetti, whom he decided to console in the South of France. Wishing that she had not cut short her stay in the United States, Simone de Beauvoir sent a cable to Algren, suggesting that she return to Chicago. He replied: 'No. Too much work'.[19] According to her autobiography, she was both distressed and relieved. Meanwhile, in correspondence with Algren, she addressed him as 'My own Nelson', 'Nelson, my only love', 'My beloved husband', telling him that 'we shall never be separated. I am your wife for ever'.[20] (So much for the woman who loathed marriage.) With such endearments, 'I made up for my going away . . . and I lied', she was to confess many years later.[21]

In June 1949, Algren arrived in Paris, and was shown the sights. By her account, he and Sartre took to each other. She introduced Algren to 'the family' and to her famous friends. Then the lovers travelled to Italy and North Africa. After spending September in Paris, they promised to meet the following year. Consequently, in August 1950, Simone de Beauvoir spent two months in Algren's house on Lake Michigan; and she again stayed with him in October 1951. But he now informed her that he intended to remarry his former wife. He could not accept the fact that he did not come first with Simone de Beauvoir — that she put Sartre and her life in Paris before him and their association. With this fifth visit, their liaison appeared to come to an end. However, they continued to write to each other. By the summer of 1952, a young Jewish journalist on *Les Temps Modernes* named Claude Lanzmann had moved into her studio apartment in the rue de la Boucherie as her lover.

When, in 1954, *Les Mandarins* appeared, Algren was not at all pleased to find his affair with the author transparently portrayed as that of Anne and Lewis, although Simone de Beauvoir had written to tell him that 'I am trying to tell *our* story. . . . I like to remember those things by writing them down'.[22] In that novel, the physical relationship was conveyed in far stronger terms than she cared to use elsewhere in fiction when alluding to unions modelled on her association with Sartre. With the publication of *La Force des choses* in 1963, where she spoke of their liaison without the disguise of fiction, Algren could not conceal his resentment: '. . . when you share the relationship with everybody who can afford a book', he declared, 'you reduce it'.[23] The hurt lingered on to the end. A few hours before his death in 1981, Algren expressed his bitterness to the noted journalist, W.J. Weatherby:

> She gave me a disguise, another name, in *Les Mandarins*, but in a later book . . . [*La Force des choses*], she tried to make our relationship into a great international literary affair, naming me and quoting from some of my letters. She must have been awfully hard up for something to write about. . . . Hell, love letters should be private. I've been in whorehouses all over the world and the women there always close the door. . . . But this woman flung the door open and called in the public and the press. . . . I don't have any malice against her, but I think it was an appalling thing to do.[24]

Whatever the offence against delicacy which offended Algren so deeply, the fact remains that Simone de Beauvoir's revelations made him an international name.

Their correspondence, interrupted after the publication of *Les Mandarins*, was resumed five years later, in 1959. Algren's passport had been withdrawn during the period of Senator McCarthy's witch hunt. As a former Communist, and a member of the committee to free Julius and Ethel Rosenberg, who were convicted of passing atomic secrets to the Russians, he had inevitably fallen under suspicion. Passions ran high among members of the French Left on the execution of the Rosenbergs. Sartre called it 'a legal lynching which covers an entire people with blood'.[25] His fury was shared by his companion.

When Nelson Algren's passport was restored to him, he arrived in Paris in the spring of 1960. Once again he stayed with Simone de Beauvoir, and they visited Spain, Greece and Turkey together. He confirmed her own condemnation of America: 'I have been swindled, duped, betrayed', he raged. 'Once I lived in America. . . . Now I live on territory occupied by Americans.'[26] Simone de Beauvoir's hatred for America as a land powerless to change, incapable of 'forging the future', pierces through *La Force des choses*, and owes not a little to Algren himself. It reaches its apogee in a notorious passage of *Tout compte fait*, where she bemoaned the defeat of such urban terrorist groups as the Black Panthers and the Weathermen, while calmly anticipating the collapse of the American economy which might bring revolution 'on a planetary scale'. True, she herself might not live long enough to witness this cataclysm, but 'it is a consoling prospect', she added, coolly disregarding the fate of all those who would inevitably perish in the creation of the longed-for revolutionary utopia.[27]

On the other side of the coin was the Soviet Union. As we have seen, the companions' prewar sympathies lay in that direction, with a society from whence they fully expected a new man, with new unalienated relationships, to arise. (Indeed, Sartre would return from Soviet Russia convinced that new relations between men had been forged there. 'Freedom of criticism is total in the USSR', he blandly declared, while so many were languishing unheard in the Gulag.)[28] However, the companions never joined the Communist Party: they constantly flirted with it, remaining illustrious fellow-travellers.

Perturbed at first by the Nazi–Soviet Pact of 1939, Simone de Beauvoir later made excuses for it. In the beginning, the French Communist Party, as a result of the Nazi–Soviet Pact, did not support the war effort. Only in 1941, when Nazi Germany invaded Russia, did the French Communists throw their weight into the Resistance movement, from which they emerged in 1944 with reputation and power greatly enhanced.

As for Sartre, now bent on a form of literature committed to political involvement, he tried at first — with David Rousset, Georges Altman and others — to promote a third force between the two superpowers through a movement called the Rassemblement Démocratique Révolutionnaire (RDR). With the growing rift between the United States and the Soviet Union, though, this group appeared to have no future, and Sartre resigned from it. The failure of the RDR led Sartre ever closer to the Communists, despite their attacks on him; and with him went Simone de Beauvoir.

One event caused some slight momentary hesitation. This was the Kravchenko affair. The Soviet defector, Victor Kravchenko, author of *I Chose Freedom*, was suing the Communist paper, *Les Lettres Françaises*, because it had declared that the real author of the book was the American secret service. Simone de Beauvoir accompanied Sartre to the hearings. Among the numerous witnesses for Kravchenko was the impressive Margarete Buber-Neumann (not Beuber-Newmann, as Simone de Beauvoir gives the name in characteristic cavalier fashion). Frau Buber-Neumann, daughter-in-law of Martin Buber, the Jewish existentialist philosopher, had later married the German Communist leader, Heinz Neumann, who was arrested in Russia in 1937 and never seen again. She herself was sentenced to five years in a Soviet labour camp in Karaganda. Then, along with other German Communists, radicals or Jews, she was handed over to Hitler after the Nazi–Soviet Pact, and transferred to Ravensbrück concentration camp. Simone de Beauvoir thought that the evidence given by Margarete Buber-Neumann sounded convincing. Moreover, it was plain to her from what other witnesses said also, that there really were labour camps in Soviet Russia. It was scarcely necessary for her to wait until 1949 to be aware of that fact. Indeed, their existence was common knowledge, at least since 1936, as she herself admits in a footnote on page 218 of *La Force des choses*.

Despite the revelations about the Soviet camps and the debate about whether to publish the truth (and so supposedly destroy the hopes of the working class), the underlying sympathies of the companions never varied during the years of the cold war. 'For the USSR, in spite of everything, was and remained the land of socialism: the revolutionary seizure of power had been accomplished', she wrote in *La Force des choses*, expressing also the opinion of Sartre. 'Even . . . if crimes had been committed, the USSR had never questioned the appropriation of the means of production; its regime differed radically from those which aim to establish or preserve the domination of a class.'[29] Thus the aim and the ideal, however perverted or bloodstained in practice, still remained unsullied. If millions were shunted around and perished in the Soviet state's pursuit of the Marxist-Leninist ideal, nevertheless, the Revolution was still incarnate in the USSR. On the other hand, for her and her companion, the Free World possessed no values but simply sustained American interests. That the USSR sustained Soviet interests was not considered.

In their view, what must be avoided at all costs was to be seen to join in anti-Soviet attacks. When Camus urged the companions to flee the Russians (war between the superpowers was believed to be imminent), they refused to move because 'we did not consider fleeing from a regime where, in spite of everything, socialism was embodied'.[30] Twice repeated, that phrase, 'in spite of everything', reveals their inadequacy in the face of human suffering that was now taking place among the underdogs of the democracies or in the so-called Third World. The Soviet Union always had to be given the benefit of the doubt, a benefit that was never extended to the democracies of the West. This might be called a form of selective compassion.

Underlying differences between Sartre and Camus, which had been present since the beginning, led to successive breaks and reconciliations between the two men. In these political divergences, Simone de Beauvoir sided with Sartre. Once, however (when Sartre was absent in the United States in 1945), she and Camus dined alone together, and afterwards they went back to her room where they talked into the small hours. He confided his personal problems to her. Despite his charm and his success with women, she later judged him to be a male chauvinist.

The final rift over Camus's book, *L'Homme révolté*, in 1951, proved to be the token of a symbolic clash between two irreconcilable standpoints. While Camus showed no particular love for the United States, he understood the delusions fostered by Soviet ideology and by messianic utopianism, and he resolutely sought to adopt a humanist and humanitarian stance. For Simone de Beauvoir, this meant merely that he assumed a moral pose and settled for 'bourgeois values'.[31] That Camus, born into the working class in Algeria, would choose to put his mother before the Algerian revolutionaries whose violence might lead to her death, failed to move the author of *Le Sang des autres*. She could declare that she was personally unaffected by the total break between the former friends.

Towards the end of *La Force des choses*, Simone de Beauvoir summed up her response to the USSR, after a visit when the companions had been treated to a verbal drubbing by the Soviet leader, Nikita Khrushchev. It made no difference: 'From the beginning of the cold war', she wrote, 'we had decided in favour of the Soviet Union; since it pursues a policy of peace and de-Stalinisation, we do not confine ourselves to preferring it: its cause, its fortunes are our own'. Compared with the technocratic society of the West, 'in the Soviet Union man is being created and if that does not occur without pain, if there are hard knocks, backslidings, mistakes, everything around him, all that happens to him, is weighty with meaning'.[32] From Boris Pasternak's epic novel of revolutionary anguish, *Doctor Zhivago*, denied publication in the USSR (a book which she said she found 'completely obscure'), or later from that shattering work, *Cancer Ward*, by Alexander Solzhenitsyn, she maintained that she learned nothing, because she was already totally familiar with Soviet life as a result of her visits there.

According to Simone de Beauvoir, if Olga Ivinskaya, beloved of the poet Boris Pasternak and model for Lara in *Doctor Zhivago*, had been sentenced to eight years forced labour, it was because she had committed foreign currency offences. The author of *L'Invitée* did not query the rightness of the sentence, nor did she consider it excessive: she merely added a footnote to the effect that only criminals were punished with internment in the labour camps. The inhabitants of the Gulag — writers, artists, seekers after freedom of expression and belief — would be unlikely to smile at such an ingenuous acceptance of Soviet propaganda.

Scarcely surprising, then, that the former camp inmate, Alexander Solzhenitsyn, unable to publish his work in his own country, would decline to meet 'the Sartres', as he called them. He complained that although they stood up for all and sundry in the West and the Third World, 'they had nothing to say about the destruction of *our* culture, . . . of *our* nation . . .'. With his formidable rhetoric and with bitter irony, Solzhenitsyn thundered: 'if the process of smothering a Russian writer not quite extinguished under Stalin continued under the collective leadership . . . this did not insult their leftist creed: if people were stifled in the land of communism, that must be what progress demanded!'[33] Simone de Beauvoir never understood why Solzhenitsyn did not want to talk with them.

From 1962 to 1966 the companions made yearly visits to the Soviet Union. True, they had not been happy about the Soviet invasion of Hungary in 1956, and had protested against it. Eventually, the treatment of certain Russian writers and intellectuals began to disturb them. The testimony of Solzhenitsyn could no longer be eluded. They were troubled when the poet Joseph Brodsky was condemned to forced labour in 1964; and two years later when the writers Andrei Sinyavsky and Yuli Daniel were sent to labour camp for publishing their writings abroad. 'What are you doing here at this time?', Ilya Ehrenburg asked the companions.[34] They took the hint and did not return.

For some twenty years these privileged literary figures had been travelling around the world as ambassadors of the conformist, 'progressive', pro-revolutionary Left. Simone de Beauvoir had written an extremely long book in defence of what was happening in Communist China and in praise of the benefits of the regime, after a brief visit there with Sartre in 1955. This was *La Longue Marche* (1957). She always felt that she could know a country by reading books, meeting intellectuals and selected individuals in key positions, and being guided around by leaders or 'experts'. Without a knowledge of the language, she ventured to criticise with asperity other Western observers who expressed doubts. As for herself, she believed in the veracity of what she was told and she took what she was shown for the whole picture. ('I did not personally see any labour camps'.)[35]

She regarded China as a special case, and she accepted

restrictions on press freedom there on the ground of revolutionary 'necessity', restrictions which she would have been quick to challenge if they had occurred in France or in other democracies. In her survey, she was patronising to the Chinese, supposedly incapable of discovering the truth for themselves: 'since the question is that of instructing illiterate masses, a degree of government control is imperative'.[36] True, she disliked the heroic commonplaces in current Chinese literature and the arts. But as with the USSR in the heyday of her admiration, in China a society directed to 'the future' was being shaped, 'a new type of man' was being created, and this utopian ideal justified conditions that she would not have tolerated for a moment at home. The important thing was that here, in China, 'a profound and authentic revolution' was taking place.[37] To say that it was 'authentic' was the highest praise.

More heady than the reception in China was the welcome extended to Sartre and Simone de Beauvoir by the revolutionary government of Cuba in 1960. All was gaiety in 'the honeymoon of the Revolution', as Sartre characterised it.[38] Fidel Castro himself took them in hand for three days. They met 'Che' Guevara, the idol and soon the martyr of the revolutionary Left. Simone de Beauvoir declared that 'the Cuban revolution is not only a success but an example'. For the first time in her life she was witnessing 'happiness that had been conquered by violence'. The execution of opponents of the regime she judged to be 'necessary'.[39] Here was an echo not only of the *épuration* but of the Jacobin Terror. How did she know that each one of these summary executions was justified?

However, when the companions returned to Cuba some months later, they found that 'the "honeymoon of the revolution" was over'.[40] Homosexuals were being persecuted, intellectuals deprived of their freedom. Worse still, in her opinion, the policies of Fidel Castro himself were not revolutionary enough: this was largely because she thought that he was no longer promoting revolution in the rest of Latin America.

During the long and bloody war waged by the Algerian Muslims to win independence from France, the companions had eventually sided with the Front de Libération Nationale (FLN) which pursued a policy of terror. They were rightly outspoken in their condemnation of torture which was being practised by certain sections of the French Army, though they did not condemn terrorist outrages committed on the Algerian side. The bombing of civilians in restaurants only reminded them of the actions of the French Resistance in derailing trains.

Simone de Beauvoir walked with Sartre in the demonstrations against General de Gaulle's return to power. With her companion she signed the 'Manifesto of the 121', joining the protesters who asserted the Frenchman's right to refuse to take up arms in the Algerian War. As a result of their support for the cause of Algerian independence, there were attempts on Sartre's life, and her own was threatened. It was the first time that the signing of manifestos and the participation in public demonstrations involved them in physical risk. She felt bitter, cut off from her compatriots who did not share her views. Only in later years did she express her disillusion with the course that the independent government of Algeria had adopted. As in other instances, she had fully expected that the victory of the revolutionaries would mean the implementation of socialism. Instead, she found the new Algerian government to be both nationalistic and reactionary, and its treatment of women deplorable.

The companions had both favoured the establishment of the state of Israel in 1948, although afterwards, through their friendship with Algerian Muslims, they tried to keep an even-handed attitude (not always successfully) between Israelis and Palestinians. Simone de Beauvoir had been influenced by her liaison with Claude Lanzmann, a keen Zionist (to become well-known for *Shoah*, his vast documentary film on the Nazi destruction of the Jewish people). Although they ceased to be lovers from 1958, they remained friends and colleagues on *Les Temps Modernes*. He accompanied Sartre and Simone de Beauvoir on their visit to Egypt and Israel (just before the Six Day War broke out in 1967). Such was the standing of the literary pair that they were received by the Egyptian President and the Israeli Prime Minister.

What engaged her whole-hearted support was the student revolt in Paris in May 1968: to her it seemed a festival without parallel. Yet it was Sartre, not she herself, who spoke at the Sorbonne when the students took over the university. She made the same excuse that she had offered for her reticence during the Second World War, declaring that her views were merely a carbon copy of his. Meanwhile, Sartre was condoning violence, employing extremist rhetoric in favour of terror. From 1968, the companions supported the young French Maoists who emerged from the student revolt. Although in their alliance with the Maoists the companions challenged the law, through their backing for such *gauchiste* papers as *La Cause du peuple* or *L'Idiot international*, they themselves, because of their eminence, were never arrested. This adoption of an ever more extreme *gauchiste* position coincided with the diminution of Sartre's influence in France.

Particularly painful to her in later years was the sense that she no longer reigned supreme. When Sartre became blind and infirm, she maintained that he had fallen under the influence of his Cairo-born Jewish secretary, Pierre Victor (pen name of Benny Lévy), who, she felt, distorted the great man's views and made him say what he did not really mean. The two remained at daggers drawn.

Then there was the question of Sartre's mistresses. She liked to give the impression that she either took lightly or was somehow reconciled to the sequence of his often 'ravishing' lady friends — 'this crazy fellow Sartre', she called him as she once listed them for Nelson Algren's benefit.[41] But a new development occurred in 1956 when he met a seventeen-year-old student of his work, Arlette El-Kaïm, who soon became his mistress. An Algerian-born Jewess, she came to occupy a large and 'serious' place in his life. When Simone de Beauvoir learned that he had asked Arlette to marry him, she is said to have complained to friends: 'He cannot do that to me'.[42] Eventually, Sartre not only legally adopted the young woman but he also made her his executor (a source of friction between her and *le Castor* after his demise). In her turn, Simone de Beauvoir legally adopted a young student admirer named Sylvie Le Bon whom she had known since 1960. They saw each other almost every day, and Sylvie accompanied her on many of her travels in later years.

When readers noted the last paragraph of *La Force des choses* they were astonished:

> Once more I see the hedge of hazel bushes shaken in the wind and the promises at which my heart leapt so madly when I glimpsed that gold mine at my feet, an entire life to be lived.

They were kept. Still, as I turn my incredulous gaze towards that credulous adolescent, I gauge with amazement how far I have been cheated.[43]

She felt 'cheated' less because she had discovered the suffering world of the underdog or because she was in despair over the war with Algeria (as she later averred), than because she could not bear the approach of old age and its ills, the thought of death, annihilation, the void, the vanity of human accomplishment.

Simone de Beauvoir came to regret having written that revealing word 'cheated', frequently protesting that the whole passage had been misunderstood. She explained at length in later interviews and writings how it was connected to a passage in *Mémoires d'une jeune fille rangée* where she had described how she stood by the hazel bushes, a girl full of hope, dreaming of fame. Yet the author had commented even there that 'no life, no moment in any life could keep the promises at which my credulous heart leapt so madly'.[44] The repetition of words and phrases was clearly meant to be like a musical reprise, part of a literary strategy that went awry — she called it 'a literary blunder'.[45] Were the promises kept, as she maintained? Some, no doubt, if not the utopian revolutionary ones. Yet no amount of protestation and explanation could call back the word 'cheated' or counteract the sense of shortcoming and betrayal.

Notes

1. Nancy Cunard , 'Letter from Paris', *Horizon*, June 1945, pp. 398–9.
2. Cyril Connolly, 'Comment', *Horizon*, May 1945, p. 295.
3. Ibid., p. 302.
4. C. Francis and F. Gontier, *Les Ecrits de Simone de Beauvoir*, p. 334.
5. *La Force de l'âge*, p. 578.
6. 'Pour une Morale de l'ambiguïté', p. 181.
7. Ibid., p. 190.
8. 'Oeil pour oeil', in *L'Existentialisme et la sagesse des nations*, Nagel, 1963, p. 127.

9. Ibid., pp. 138, 143.
10. *La Force des choses*, pp. 31–3.
11. Mamaine Koestler, 1 November 1946, *Living with Koestler. Mamaine Koestler's Letters 1945–51*, ed. Celia Goodman, Weidenfeld & Nicolson, 1985, p. 43.
12. Ibid. (26 February 1949), p. 100.
13. C. Francis and F. Gontier, *Simone de Beauvoir*, p. 251.
14. Arthur and Cynthia Koestler, *Stranger on the Square*, Hutchinson, 1984, pp. 71–2.
15. *La Force des choses*, p. 82.
16. *America Day by Day*, tr. Patrick Dudley, Duckworth, 1952, p. 77.
17. Mary McCarthy, 'Mlle Gulliver en Amérique' (1952), in idem, *The Humanist in the Bathtub*, Signet, 1964, p. 23.
18. Nelson Algren, *The Man with the Golden Arm* (1949), Cedric Chivers, Bath, 1972, p. 22.
19. *La Force des choses*, p. 179.
20. C. Francis and F. Gontier, *Simone de Beauvoir*, pp. 267–8.
21. Ibid., p. 274 note.
22. Ibid., p. 288.
23. Quoted by Axel Madsen, *Hearts and Minds. The Common Journey of Simone de Beauvoir and Jean-Paul Sartre*, Morrow, 1977, p. 140.
24. W.J. Weatherby, 'The Last Interview', in Nelson Algren, *The Devil's Stocking*, Arbor, 1983, pp. 10–11.
25. Sartre in *Libération*, 22 March 1953, quoted in Raymond Aron, *Mémoires*, p. 308.
26. *La Force des choses*, p. 218.
27. *Tout compte fait*, p. 465.
28. Sartre in *Libération*, 14–20 July 1954, quoted in Michel-Antoine Burnier, *Les Existentialistes et la politique*, Collection Idées, Gallimard, 1966, p. 99.
29. *La Force des choses*, p. 518.
30. Ibid., p. 252.
31. Ibid., p. 279.
32. Ibid., p. 667.
33. Alexander Solzhenitsyn, *The Oak and the Calf*, tr. Harry Willetts, Collins / Harvill, 1980, p. 119 and note 4, p. 149.
34. *Tout compte fait*, p. 357.
35. *The Long March*, tr. A. Wainhouse, Deutsch and Weidenfeld & Nicolson, 1958, p. 384.
36. Ibid., p. 315.
37. Ibid., pp. 479, 483, 501.
38. *La Force des choses*, p. 515.
39. 'Où en est la Révolution cubaine?', 7 April 1960, in C. Francis and F. Gontier, *Les Ecrits de Simone de Beauvoir*, p. 190; also *La Force des choses*, pp. 485, 515.
40. *La Force des choses*, p. 596.
41. C. Francis and F. Gontier, *Simone de Beauvoir*, p. 274.

42. Axel Madsen, *Hearts and Minds*, p. 206.
43. *La Force des choses*, p. 686.
44. *Mémoires d'une jeune fille rangée*, p. 148.
45. Francis Jeanson, 'Entretiens avec Simone de Beauvoir', in *Simone de Beauvoir ou l'enterprise de vivre*, p. 271.

6 Feminism: Old and New

The book which made Simone de Beauvoir a household name — even to those who merely glanced through its 972 pages, or its five-page-long paragraphs — was *Le Deuxième Sexe*, published in two volumes in June and November 1949. It radically changed the whole manner of looking at the condition of women; and its influence soon spread for good or ill beyond France throughout the entire field of culture. Several generations of writers and researchers have gained sustenance from its material and the manner of its approach.

The first volume, subtitled 'Facts and Myths', was well received: it was the second volume, subtitled 'Living Experience', which caused a commotion. Today, it is difficult to comprehend the uproar (except possibly in terms of the virulent anti-woman debates that have raged at various intervals through the ages). In France in 1949, such themes as a girl's sexual initiation, female sexuality, lesbianism, abortion, birth control, were not treated openly in works addressed to the general reading public, and least of all by a woman novelist who spoke out plainly and directly. Since then, some women writers have not hesitated to vie with their masculine colleagues in crudity of language. The drive to be ever more provocative and sensational has made Simone de Beauvoir's writing appear discreet in comparison with theirs.

Things were different in 1949. Catholics were in the forefront of the opposition, and the book was placed on the Index of forbidden works. The Catholic novelist, François Mauriac, did not mince his words when he told one of her colleagues on *Les Temps Modernes*: 'I've learned everything there is to know about your boss's vagina'.[1] Communists together with Leftists of various persuasions attacked the book. In private, Camus charged her with pouring ridicule on the French male. She received letters signed by 'very active members of the first sex', and by similar would-be wits. Some of these, after calling her frustrated and frigid, a neurotic virago, a nymphomaniac, a lesbian, graciously offered to cure her condition, whatever it might be. She was astonished by the low tone of mockery. At the same time, she began to hear from female letter-writers. Her continuing correspondence with them was to give her a further insight into the experience of women in different walks of life.

It is vital to realise what the book is, and what it is not. Despite its allusions to history, *Le Deuxième Sexe* does not offer a straightforward or traditional account of woman's fate and, indeed, it is often weakest on that score. What the work does is to present the reader with the first attempt to examine the position of women in terms of Sartre's existentialist philosophy. In February 1940, Sartre had remarked in his notebooks that: 'The whole question [of woman] needs to be re-examined'.[2] When, after the War, Simone de Beauvoir was looking for a subject and wondering about what being a woman had actually meant to her — though she insisted as ever that her career had not been at all impeded by her sex — Sartre observed: 'All the same, you weren't brought up in the same way as a boy: you should look into it more closely'.[3] The work that resulted from her enquiry, inspired and encouraged by Sartre, is not original in its philosophical outlook but in its application of Sartrian existentialism to the subject of woman.

Simone de Beauvoir makes her attitude quite clear from the outset: 'The viewpoint we are adopting is that of existentialist ethics'.[4] This outlook is founded on total freedom and on action. To paraphrase Sartre broadly: the thing that counts is what man through his deeds makes of what the world has made of him. The idea is that each person seeks fulfilment as a complete autonomous human being. As Simone de Beauvoir put it: whenever the individual falls back in the effort, the fall is a moral fault if the person consents to it. But failure can be the consequence of action by others, or oppression. In either case, the result is bad. The entire criticism of women's attitudes in the book, criticism which has even given rise to the charge of misogyny, is in fact rooted in the notion that, by consenting in various ways to the image that men have of them, women commit a grave fault. Yet in so far as the present position of woman is due to male oppression, her situation resembles that of other victims of tyranny, such as Blacks, workers or colonial subjects.

She goes on to state: 'Now what defines the situation of women in a remarkable way is that while being an autonomous freedom, along with every human creature, she discovers herself and chooses herself in a world where men oblige her to accept herself as the Other . . .'.[5] It is man, entrenched in his dominant position of privilege and superiority, who regards himself as the essential being; and he views woman as the inessential being (or the Other). How, then, asks Simone de Beauvoir, can a woman attain to full humanity? What circumstances are setting limits to the freedom of woman and can she move beyond them? The thesis is posed by Simone de Beauvoir solely in existentialist terms, while she seeks a way out of the impasse in which women find themselves denied freedom and fulfilment as autonomous human beings. *Le Deuxième Sexe* is thus primarily a work of theory, analysis ('an attempt at lucidity'), and interpretation, though one which ultimately and inevitably challenges the existing order. Women are expected to draw certain conclusions from the negative picture which will enable them to see things differently and to act in accordance with their own interest. (All this should benefit men, too, in the end, it is suggested.) And so it was to prove.

The freshness of this approach lies in the fact that the condition of one half of humanity is being studied in all its aspects, and treated consistently by a woman writer in a large work and on the basis of a single philosophical theory. The theme is not simply presented in the form of responses to particular events or injustices. Moreover, here was a woman novelist who brought to bear on the subject a whole range of evidence drawn from the writings of physiologists, biologists, cultural anthropologists, psychiatrists, political economists. Some of this material may well now be outdated, but the mere act of bringing it together in one place was an important contribution in itself at the time. After examining these sources, Simone de Beauvoir declined to accept the concept of woman's place and function as presented by leading biologists; nor would she adhere either to the historical materialism of Engels or (after Sartre) to Freudian psychology.

The main conclusion she drew from the history of women was that it had been 'made by men'. (One of the epigraphs to the first volume was taken from the seventeenth-century writer Poulain de La Barre, who said: 'Everything written about women by men should be treated with care because they are the judges in their own case'.)[6] It was less her sketchy account of the history of women than her examination of the myths surrounding the second sex that would prove highly suggestive and influential. To show how men tend to see women she discussed the work of a number of leading writers, including Henry de Montherlant and D.H. Lawrence. Her attack upon the pernicious attitudes of some masculine writers found its mark, and would later inspire Kate Millett's savage analysis of the work of Henry Miller and Norman Mailer in *Sexual Politics*. Similarly, Simone de Beauvoir's insights into the role of woman as Eve or Madonna, or as the personification of institutions, would serve as a precedent for the detailed analyses of feminine myths by Marina Warner.

The whole drive of *Le Deuxième Sexe* is to undermine the deep-rooted myths about women, and to destroy the notion of 'the Eternal Feminine', the idea (so convenient for men) of what is supposedly characteristic of woman, limited to her and properly suited only to her. The important question Simone de Beauvoir asks herself is: what precisely is woman (or man)? The answer she gives, in accordance with Sartrian existentialism, is nothing to start with: 'A living being is nothing else but what it does . . . essence does not precede existence: in its pure subjectivity, the human being *is nothing*'.[7] On the vexed question of nature or nurture, Simone de Beauvoir follows Sartre in opting for the latter; and she insists that the whole idea of what is feminine is a construct of education and culture down the centuries.

Surely men would be more sensible to reject the myth and to engage in an 'authentic relationship with an autonomous being', she rightly suggests. Still, she recognises that it is immensely difficult for women themselves to reconcile the desired state of autonomous individual with their 'female destiny'.[8] How simpler it is for them to yield to slavery rather than to struggle to free themselves, declares Simone de Beauvoir, the advocate of conquering one's own fate and winning one's own freedom. The heavy irony marks an attempt to rouse the majority of the women of her day from their torpor.

The whole of the second volume of *Le Deuxième Sexe* is devoted to an analysis of the actual experience of woman from childhood to old age. The evidence is drawn from multifarious sources: from Stekel on frigidity in women, from the Kinsey Report, from Havelock Ellis; from women writers, including Colette (whom she once visited), Virginia Woolf, Rosamond Lehmann, Katherine Mansfield, Dorothy Parker; from the life stories of great writers which revealed, for example, the misery of Countess Tolstoy, locked in frustrated conflict with a difficult husband of genius. True, Freud used literary sources for his psychological interpretations. A similar procedure had been adopted by the Freudian psychiatrist, Helene Deutsch, in her study, *The Psychology of Woman* (1944), a work known to Simone de Beauvoir, who used it to much effect. However, as a psychiatrist Helene Deutsch was writing chiefly for students and scholars in her field, whereas Simone de Beauvoir aimed to reach a wider audience, and succeeded in doing so. The cultural mix of *Le Deuxième Sexe* — whether or not the reader agrees with various details that fall within his or her competence — remains impressive.

Examining the life of women as actually lived, Simone de Beauvoir encapsulated the existentialist notion that existence precedes essence in the now celebrated formula: 'You are not born a woman: you become one'.[9] Childhood conditioning, sexual initiation (generally tough), these subjects lead toward the situation of the married woman, where all is gloom. Fundamentally, Simone de Beauvoir sees marriage in the light of her parents' union, or rather disunion. For her it takes the form commonly practised by the French bourgeoisie in her day.

Love and marriage are still as incompatible, in her eyes, as they were for the medieval troubadours. The very principle of marriage is nothing less than 'obscene', she declares, because an exchange which should be founded on spontaneity is transformed into one based on rights and duties.[10] The wife becomes enslaved in demeaning and unpaid household tasks, and in childbearing, dwindling progressively into a less interesting person — a theme that has been treated *ad nauseam* by women writers since *Le Deuxième Sexe*, but one which was not then a commonplace. Meanwhile, the husband (whose burdens as responsible parent go unmentioned) enjoys all the privileges of economic autonomy. In addition, he is free and can be unfaithful with impunity.

As for motherhood, it is one more nail in the woman's coffin. Maternity can 'ruin' a woman's professional life, Simone de Beauvoir affirms, expatiating on the need for birth control and legal abortion.[11] Only too often abandoned by the husband when the children are grown up, the middle-aged wife gains her freedom at a time when she does not know what to do with it. In short, it is not to Simone de Beauvoir that one will go to find the portrait of a marriage between equals devoted to each other, or any true appreciation of the positive aspects of family life.

Counterbalancing her harsh condemnation of marriage and family is the notion of 'a pact' between a man and a woman who would live in freedom and sincerity. Such an arrangement alone would abolish the drawbacks of marriage, in her (not entirely frank) opinion. This 'pact' immediately recalls the one between Sartre and Simone de Beauvoir — a contract whose terms would not become known until the publication of *La Force de l'âge* in 1961, where the author herself was to indicate some of the limitations and liabilities of this arrangement.

Only work can ensure economic freedom for the woman, a theme which the creator of *Le Deuxième Sexe* would reiterate throughout her life with renewed emphasis. The value of work for a woman's self-esteem, self-confidence and independence, is pre-eminent. If the work in question is of a kind that the woman enjoys — a profession, say, which brings economic freedom and even fame, as in Simone de Beauvoir's case — that is no doubt true. It may be questioned, however, whether monotonous tasks performed in factories would bring quite the same psychological, social and financial rewards.

The author projects the vision of 'the free woman' who, she insists, is not to be taken for the woman of easy virtue. However, she seems to regret that, unlike a man, a free woman cannot find casual partners in the street without courting danger. (One is reminded of Simone de Beauvoir's risky exploits as a young girl, as related in *Mémoires d'une jeune fille rangée*.) Above all, the free woman as conceived by Simone de Beauvoir is emancipated through work, not the vote. Yet such a woman, too, encounters problems: in reconciling her 'femininity' with her career, for instance — and here, the author's acceptance of a desirable 'femininity' appears to contradict her insistence elsewhere that there is no such thing as a feminine essence. In any event, such privileged free women are still 'only half way' — and in that observation can be heard an echo of George Sand's complaint to her fellow-writer Hortense Allart in 1851, to the effect that their own conduct, as 'artists' who pursued free love and who could 'live almost as men do', had not brought them contentment as women. In Simone de Beauvoir's opinion, women as a whole still had to strive for their own emancipation. Only in a socialist world, she suggested, would women attain 'perfect liberation'.[12]

The author of *Le Deuxième Sexe* did not appear to realise that this dream of female fulfilment through socialist utopia was strictly nothing new. Yet she was aware of the Saint-Simonians. Throughout the nineteenth century, from the utopian socialist followers of comte Henri de Saint-Simon onwards, who linked feminism and socialism together, there was scarcely a woman writer of any significance in France who did not follow suit. The cause of women and that of the workers became one cause from George Sand and Flora Tristan to Louise Colet and beyond. For many, too, this cause would be linked with the emancipation of the Blacks. Nor did George Sand place any greater faith in the vote than the author of *Le Deuxième Sexe*: they both wanted to see women function as complete human beings; and they both strove above all for a change in consciousness on the part of men and women.

So it is that Simone de Beauvoir often appears both superficial and unjust where her feminine predecessors are concerned. Her own youthful indifference to the long-drawn-out struggle for female political emancipation — women did not obtain the vote in France until 1945 — remained constant. In her discussion of her literary forerunners, she overlooked the considerable political radiance of Mme de Staël, and the way in which the creator of *Corinne* opened a path for women writers. Moreover, Simone de Beauvoir made no mention of the huge debt owed to George Sand, of whose wide-ranging influence and innovatory qualities she apparently remained unaware. Despite her own liking for the work of George Eliot, of Virginia Woolf or of Colette, she maintained that there had never been any geniuses among women writers — a view that has since been resoundingly contested. (Indeed, that severe critic F.R. Leavis placed George Eliot in 'the great tradition' of English novelists in 1948, just before Simone de Beauvoir's study was published.)

Evidently, *Le Deuxième Sexe*, despite its theorising and its air of objectivity, is a deeply personal work. As Simone de Beauvoir was to admit near the end of her life, it expressed '*my* vision of woman. That was how *I* had experienced it'.[13] A certain distaste for the body, its viscous secretions, its functions (a disgust to be found in Sartre also), is particularly striking. Neither of them wanted to have children. She believed that motherhood would interfere with her career as a writer ('I thought I couldn't have children because I wanted to write', she once owned);[14] and he desired neither the burden nor the responsibility. Although she granted that some women might find fulfilment in motherhood, she herself resented and fought against the myth-making that surrounds maternity. Nobody ever asked Sartre whether he felt unfulfilled because he was not a father, she would complain.

However, her opposition to marriage and motherhood as feminine dead ends is rooted in her experience of life in her social class. Her condemnation of women who limit their options and who destroy themselves for love, derived not only from the fate of her friend Zaza but from that of one of her fellow-teachers at Rouen, known as 'Louise Perron' in *La Force de l'âge*. This was Renée Ballon, so infatuated with André Malraux (or 'J.B.' in that volume), that her wits were turned.[15] Simone de Beauvoir did not want a woman to put all her gifts into love for a man. She wanted risk and adventure, and struggled to conquer them for herself. Consequently, the denial of risk and adventure to women, their all-too-ready acceptance of a limited horizon and limited expectations, seemed to her a serious deprivation. She transposed her own struggle into that of women in general.

As for the fate of the middle-aged woman, all too often left to her own devices by her husband or lover, this was not only the fate of her own mother, but also to some extent that of the author herself, as Sartre in his emotional immaturity went on 'falling in love' with younger women. Fortunately, the creator of *L'Invitée* had other resources, including the enduring intellectual collaboration with her life-long companion, but these were given to relatively few women at the moment when she was writing *Le Deuxième Sexe*. Hence the stress upon career and work as a source of self-respect as well as economic independence for women. In her view, men are bound to be unfaithful. Because she does not conceive, either in her theoretical writings or her novels, the possibility of a mature, loyal and lasting relationship within marriage and family, she blandly proposes that these institutions will have to be destroyed, although she does not know what to put in their place.

From the publication of *Le Deuxième Sexe* onwards, Simone de Beauvoir never ceased to be preoccupied with the subject of woman's fate in contemporary society. While she never again published a large work on the theme, she wrote articles and prefaces (like the introduction to *La Bâtarde*, an autobiographical narrative by Violette Leduc, whom she did much to encourage); and she also gave numerous interviews where she expatiated upon it.

One of the most significant of her interpretations of the modern or free woman, an essay which pursued the permissiveness adumbrated in *Le Deuxième Sexe*, was 'Brigitte Bardot and the Lolita Syndrome', published in the American magazine *Esquire* in 1959. Here, she connected the popular French film star with Vladimir Nabokov's nymphet Lolita as an image of the ambiguous, androgynous child-woman. The naturalness of Brigitte Bardot, advertised as 'the sex kitten', her rejection of all the constraints of fashion, are seen to affirm that woman stands as 'the equal of man'. In Simone de Beauvoir's view, the eroticism of Brigitte Bardot 'is aggressive. . . . The male is an object for her, just as she is an object for him. And this is exactly what wounds masculine pride'.[16] Above all, the type of character that Brigitte Bardot sought to embody on and off the screen was in reaction against long-standing taboos, especially those which denied 'sexual autonomy' to women.

Alongside the theme of sexual freedom and equality, there was that of the injustices endured by women at work, whether in performing unpaid household tasks or in employment outside the home. Many, too, were seen to suffer in attempting to reconcile family and career. 'The most balanced women I have met', Simone de Beauvoir ventured to proclaim in an article entitled 'La Condition féminine', published in *La Nef* in 1961, 'were in China' (where, it will be remembered, she had spent a few weeks in the autumn of 1955).[17] Professional Chinese women, she asserted, actually felt no inner conflict between their career and their private life. Moreover, they were regarded as equals and treated as such by their male compatriots. This audacious generalisation about the new Chinese mentality verges on the absurd when based on a few weeks' enquiry, and it is in any case unverifiable. None the less, it indicates what the author's desired ideal still was, over a decade after the publication of *Le Deuxième*

Sexe: a socialist society that would produce a hitherto non-existent equilibrium for women. It shows how she really believed that such perfect balance was attainable through social ordering. She had seen the future and it worked.

Still, while she wanted an improvement on these lines in France, she did not see it happening there. On the contrary, conditions in what she regarded as a false democracy seemed to her to show no advance whatsoever since 1949. Meanwhile, in the United States, women had been reading *Le Deuxième Sexe* in translation, viewing her as a pioneer, as a kind of guide and guru, and they had been profiting in various ways from the insights provided by her book. Soon, with the rise of the militant feminist movement, some groups passed beyond her, and were criticising her for not being an activist. Simone de Beauvoir was well aware of the feminist revolt across the Atlantic, though she disliked what she called the attitude of 'challenge' to men (as displayed, for instance, by SCUM, the Society for Cutting Up Men). She found it absurd to treat man as the enemy, and so to have to give up living with him. This was not true feminism; it was not a way of 'living one's situation in authenticity', she told Francis Jeanson in 1966.[18]

Already, by 1966, there was some evolution in her own conception of the link between feminism and socialism. As she remarked in a lecture, 'Situation de la femme aujourd'hui', in Japan in September of that year, socialism did not now appear to her to be 'a sufficient condition' to make woman the equal of man. In countries like the Soviet Union and Poland, women were still inferior; for instance, with a few exceptions they did not occupy leading political and administrative posts. All the same, she still believed that work gave Russian women a sort of dignity, a share in public life, and a relationship with the self 'which I have not encountered in other countries'. She maintained that '[if] socialism is not a sufficient condition, it is certainly a necessary condition'.[19] Yet only a few years later she would completely reverse her attitude to socialism as a prerequisite for the equality of women with men.

To the German writer, Alice Schwarzer, in 1972, she complained that Soviet women were to be found working primarily in the less-esteemed professions. And she took as an example the invaluable Dr Ludmila Afanasyevna in Solzhenitsyn's novel

Cancer Ward who, after an exhausting day in the hospital, has to wait in queues in the shops and perform household tasks 'in exactly the same way as in other countries. And perhaps even more than in France, where a woman in a similar situation would have domestic help. . . . The conclusion to be drawn is that equality between men and women is not at all a reality in the USSR either'. The reason for this belated insight is that 'socialist countries are not really socialist; nowhere has a form of socialism been implemented which would change man as Marx desired'.[20] The traditional rôles of men and women persist. The prejudices of patriarchy were going to outlive the end of capitalism, a disillusioned Simone de Beauvoir would tell another interviewer, the English journalist Caroline Moorehead.[21]

Even the men who belonged to Leftist parties in France did not treat women well: they, too, expected their women colleagues to brew the coffee, regarding them as servants. 'I thought the victory of women would be linked to the advent of socialism. Well, socialism is a dream', she could admit to Pierre Viansson-Ponté in 1978. Her concept of it remained utopian, but she could no longer envisage 'real socialism' in the world as she knew it.[22]

What had happened to modify Simone de Beauvoir's attitude? It was not just the militant feminist upheaval in the United States and elsewhere, but the growth of a radical feminist movement in France, known as the Mouvement de Libération des Femmes (MLF), or Women's Liberation Movement after the American model. Some of its members approached Simone de Beauvoir towards the end of 1970. They were dissatisfied with the bill on abortion that was due to come before the French National Assembly, and they wanted to set in motion a campaign for free abortion on demand. The idea was to obtain the signatures of well-known women who, with others, would declare that they had broken the law and had undergone an abortion. All this appealed to Simone de Beauvoir. She had urged a change in the law in *Le Deuxième Sexe*, where she had protested against the hypocrisy that surrounded the subject. In addition, she had published a searing account of a back-street abortion in her novel, *Le Sang des autres*.

For her, it was not a question of introducing or encouraging abortions (as some people pretended), since almost a million of them were said to take place in France every year. She simply wanted decent and safe conditions for all those women, including the underprivileged, who had to undergo the operation. Doubtless, as she often remarked, she would have preferred the widespread use of methods of birth control; but given the situation as it stood, women must be saved from humiliation and physical danger. Her signature on the 'Manifesto of the 343' (published in 1971), along with that of French film stars, secretaries and housewives, marked her beginnings as a militant feminist. It meant that she had broken the law and was challenging the authorities to arrest her (just as she had challenged them with Sartre through her public support for two banned *gauchiste* newspapers the previous year).

In November 1971 she marched through Paris with women who were calling for free contraception and abortion on demand, chanting slogans and singing the 'Internationale' — 'a joyous festivity', she called it, ever responsive to the revolution as fun.[23] She joined other members of the MLF who occupied the Collège du Plessis-Robinson, a school for very young unmarried mothers, where conditions struck her as appalling. These pregnant girls, aged between twelve and eighteen, had been expelled from their own schools, and were now receiving a poor education. They were on hunger strike. 'By what code do you judge that it is a mistake to have sexual relations at thirteen?', she challenged the university vice-chancellor responsible for schools, as she made an issue of society's distaste for juvenile sexuality.[24] There spoke the advocate of sexual freedom and of greater permissiveness, the woman who had neither experienced the anxieties of a parent nor felt any empathy with them.

She helped to found an association called 'Choisir', along with the novelist Christiane Rochefort, the film actress Delphine Seyrig, and two eminent Nobel prizewinners for medicine, Jacques Monod and François Jacob. It aimed to provide legal aid for those charged with undergoing or performing abortions. The association's first president was Simone de Beauvoir herself, who acted as defence witness at the trial of a seventeen-year-old girl accused of having had an abortion. In 1974, the author of *Le Deuxième Sexe* became president of the League for Women's Rights, founded by the MLF to enlighten women about their legal position, and to denounce sexual discrimination in all its forms, at work and in writings. The idea for this body was her own. She had already started a feminist column in *Les Temps Modernes*, where she campaigned to make 'sexism' or sexual discrimination a punishable offence like racism.

Much of this feminist activity was taking place during the long period of Sartre's physical decline, when she shared the task of caring for him with his numerous women friends; and it was to continue after his death in 1980. She aimed to be provocative in order to be heard; and at first she seriously hoped that the militant feminist movement would somehow contrive to overturn established society and government. In this respect, she had not changed.

One of her American admirers, Betty Friedan, author of *The Feminine Mystique*, who felt thrilled to call on her, went away with a flea in her ear, while leaving for posterity an important record of two irreconcilable points of view. Betty Friedan had read *Le Deuxième Sexe* in the 1950s, and its existentialist perspective had made a deep impression upon her, as upon so many women throughout the world. 'It was *The Second Sex* that introduced me to that approach to reality and political responsibility — that, in effect, freed me from the rubrics of authoritative ideology and led me to whatever original analysis of women's existence I have been able to contribute', wrote Betty Friedan in *It Changed My Life*.[25]

As a pragmatist, however, the American writer was astonished to hear Simone de Beauvoir express disdain for advances in women's status in employment or for their attainment of positions of leadership. How else could women obtain the skills that would give them a voice in changing the system?, enquired Betty Friedan. Simone de Beauvoir's reply was short: 'One must simply destroy the system'. In her own day, observed the author of *Le Deuxième Sexe*, 'there was no feminism' (a statement so unfair as to beggar belief, unless she meant militant feminism of the post-1968 variety). Now, women do not want a place in society as it exists today, they want to overturn it, she averred. Those in high positions, including women in government, are merely token females ('femmes-alibis') and they should all resign to take modest posts, for instance in school-teaching. As for women journalists, they should not sign their articles, in order to demonstrate their rejection of masculine ideas of ambition and competition. When Betty Friedan asked her whether she herself was no longer going to sign her own work, she replied: 'No, of course not, because I was formed differently . . . and what I have achieved I am going to use'.[26] Very perceptively, Betty Friedan saw how the attack on so-called elitism worked to undermine democratic structures and the democratic process.

The American writer sought to use the political openings available in a parliamentary democracy to advance the cause of women. Simone de Beauvoir told her that she herself was not interested in politics: 'Personally, I do not vote'.[27] This was in 1975, and it was not strictly true. She was to admit to Alice Schwarzer that she had sometimes 'voted Communist' after the Second World War.[28] Later, she would own to the same interviewer that she had voted for the Socialist leader, François Mitterand (although Sartre advised 'revolutionary abstention'). By the time Mitterand became President of France in 1981 she could declare (after Sartre's death) that she was 'against violent, bloody revolution, at the present time at least. The price would be too high'.[29] The Socialist victory of 1981 thus modified considerably the views of this one-time follower of Sartrian revolutionary violence, who had urged women to defend themselves 'by means of violence' against masculine aggression.[30] Despite her poor opinion of such ministers for women's affairs as Françoise Giroud, she accepted an invitation from one of them, Yvette Roudy, to sit on a committee for women and culture, soon to be known as the Beauvoir committee. She was also welcomed at the Elysée by President Mitterand, although she declined to be decorated with the Légion d'honneur.[31]

Simone de Beauvoir's pioneering existentialist analysis of woman's fate in *Le Deuxième Sexe* was soon outstripped by others in succeeding generations who made use of it as the starting-point for their own work. The more extreme factions in the post-1968 militant feminist movement could criticise her for not going far enough; for not being more strongly inimical to men; for lauding not only her union with Sartre but his intellectual superiority, while urging equality between the sexes. As so often happens with pioneers, they end by seeming too mild to take their views to a logical and practical conclusion.

Towards the end of her life, however, Simone de Beauvoir caught up with the activists. She always had her own extremist attitudes on marriage, motherhood and family, for instance, and on the need to reject and overthrow the existing order, regardless of what would replace it. Only in her very last years, when into her seventies, and after Sartre's death, did she appear to be partially reconciled with the Socialist government in power in France.

Yet while speaking about the hardships suffered by the female proletariat in the abstract, she declined to appreciate the practical value of gradual advances in conditions, status and rewards for working women. She never really understood that political power could be used to serve the ends one desired — to her, that was mere 'bourgeois liberalism' and reformism. It was all or nothing, now or never. With a kind of spiritual absolutism preserved from her Catholic childhood, she wanted the absolute perfection of the ideal — something to be striven for, no doubt, but scarcely likely to be attained overnight in an imperfect world.

Notes

1. *La Force des choses*, p. 205.
2. Sartre, *Les Carnets de la drôle de guerre*, Gallimard, 1983, p. 342.
3. *La Force des choses*, p. 109.
4. *Le Deuxième Sexe*, Gallimard, 1949, vol. 1, p. 31.
5. Ibid.
6. Ibid., p. 7, epigraph; also p. 216.
7. Ibid., p. 388.
8. Ibid., p. 395.
9. Ibid., vol. 2, p. 13.
10. Ibid., p. 225.
11. Ibid., p. 539; also pp. 290ff.
12. Ibid., p. 522.
13. Alice Schwarzer, *Simone de Beauvoir To-day: Conversations 1972–1982*, tr. Marianne Howarth, Chatto & Windus/Hogarth Press, 1984, p. 109.
14. Betty Friedan, 'A Dialogue with Simone de Beauvoir' (1975), in

idem, *It Changed My Life: Writings on the Women's Movement*, Gollancz, 1977, p. 166.

15. *La Force de l'âge*, pp. 173ff.; also C. Francis and F. Gontier, *Simone de Beauvoir*, pp. 153–4.
16. 'Brigitte Bardot and the Lolita Syndrome' (1959), in C. Francis and F. Gontier, *Les Ecrits de Simone de Beauvoir*, p. 369; see also p. 375.
17. 'La Condition féminine', ibid., p. 407.
18. F. Jeanson, *Simone de Beauvoir ou l'enterprise de vivre*, p. 264; see also *Tout compte fait*, p. 502.
19. 'Situation de la femme aujourd'hui' (1966), in *Les Ecrits de Simone de Beauvoir*, pp. 437–8.
20. 'Le femme révoltée' (1972), interview with Alice Schwarzer, ibid., pp. 483–4.
21. Interview with Caroline Moorehead (1), *The Times*, 15 May 1974.
22. Interview with Pierre Viansson-Ponté, *Le Monde*, 11 January 1978.
23. *Tout compte fait*, pp. 493–4.
24. Ibid., p. 495.
25. Betty Friedan, *It Changed My Life*, p. 157.
26. Ibid., pp. 158, 162–3, 165.
27. Ibid., p. 168.
28. Alice Schwarzer, *Simone de Beauvoir To-day*, p. 101.
29. Ibid., p. 119.
30. 'La femme révoltée', interview with Alice Schwarzer, in *Les Ecrits de Simon de Beauvoir*, p. 496.
31. C. Francis and F. Gontier, *Simone de Beauvoir*, pp. 381, 389 note.

7 The Metaphysical Novel

From her beginnings as a writer, Simone de Beauvoir wanted to be a novelist. What sort of novel did she wish to write? That was precisely what she had to discover; and it took her quite a long time to find her way to what she would call 'the metaphysical novel'.

She tells how she had her own concept of art before she met Sartre in 1929. It already entailed a certain suspicion about the merits of 'realism', as she found it in the novels she read by Zola and Maupassant and their followers. This was not surprising, for she was drawn to Surrealism and abstract art. When she was about eighteen, she began work on an autobiographical novel. A year later, in 1927, she was trying to write a novel about a young girl who rebelled against her milieu — another autobiographical theme. She had therefore begun her apprenticeship as a novelist well before she encountered Sartre.

At least four further attempts were to be made before she published *L'Invitée* in 1943. In the first of these she was under the spell of Rosamond Lehmann and especially of Alain-Fournier's *Le Grand Meaulnes*. And so there was to be mystery and a sense of magic: an old mansion, a young girl who lived with her unhappy father and who met three handsome young men who were staying nearby. Eighteen months were spent on this novel which she eventually abandoned.

There followed an effort to deal with the fate of her friend Zaza in fiction, a work which engaged the budding novelist from 1931 to 1932. 'I was beginning to have something to say', Simone de Beauvoir would write later.[1] This book was built around two women, and treated the theme of 'the mirage of the Other' (which would play so important a role in *L'Invitée*), a notion central to Sartre's developing philosophy. Her novel was therefore moving towards the conception and structure that would characterise her mature writings. Its main fault, in Simone de Beauvoir's later view, was that it was too far removed from the actual circumstances on which the story was based and which gave the subject some sense of reality.

Yet another assault on fiction occupied her for two years from 1932 onwards. This was to be a large, ambitious work, with Stendhal as her principal model. It would depict an individual's revolt against bourgeois society, very like her own. In portraying French mores after the 1914–18 War she intended to expose the misdeeds of the bourgeoisie. Her private attitudes were to be shared between a brother and sister, based on Stendhal's Julien Sorel and on his Lamiel. This kind of double viewpoint would be repeated through Anne and Henri in *Les Mandarins*. The author tried to adopt a satirical tone. The plot turned to melodrama: the hero died by the guillotine (after Julien Sorel), while his beloved took poison. Dissatisfied with this melodramatic conclusion in the Romantic manner, Simone de Beauvoir tried another. The hero now associated with Communists, but could not quite share their standpoint, since he preferred humanist values. His sister fell in love with a Communist. Another figure, again based on Zaza, met her death. It seemed to the struggling novelist that the book's themes and episodes did not cohere.

There followed *Quand prime le spirituel* (*When Things of the Spirit Come First*) whose title alludes ironically to a work by the highly influential neo-Thomist philosopher, Jacques Maritain, *La Primauté du spirituel*. The whole point of Simone de Beauvoir's new attempt at fiction, begun in 1935, was that reliance on religious faith, on the sublime and 'the spirit', was a trap and a form of self-deception. This criticism of 'bourgeois' spirituality remained very close to her appreciation of her own progress and development as a young girl. The book was rejected by two publishers in 1937, and it did not appear in print until 1979. It consists of five loosely interconnected narratives through which five young women reveal themselves. Once again, the author strives to portray Zaza's fate in 'Anne', without being greatly satisfied with her treatment of the subject. The attempt to convey lies, self-deception, 'bad faith' through 'Chantal's Diary' was to be repeated in her later novels and stories.

The author relied on her own experiences at her Catholic school for 'Lisa'. She satirised in 'Marcelle' her contact with the Catholic association for workers' education, known as the Equipes sociales, led by Robert Garric — she herself had worked there when she was eighteen. Marcelle already responds to the grim sufferings of the workers, both men and women, 'and seems to carry on her shoulders the entire suffering of the world' (a theme that echoes throughout Simone de Beauvoir's mature work).[2] In the fifth narrative, 'Marguerite', she alludes to some of her own adventures as a young girl in Left Bank dance-halls and bars. When Denis, the character modelled on her cousin Jacques, returns to his wife, Marguerite learns to face facts, without relying on divine revelation or established values: 'I had to reinvent everything for myself . . .'.[3] In spite of the links between the various narratives in which some of the characters reappear, the work seems more like a collection of short stories than a novel.

From these early and renewed struggles with the fictional form, from her discussions with Sartre and her critical contribution to the long reworking of his *Melancholia*, the book which finally became *La Nausée*, Simone de Beauvoir's concept of the novel began to take shape. Like Sartre, she rejected the 'realist' or 'psychological' novel with omniscient narrator and consistent characters. Although both of them made much of this rejection in their theoretical writings, it was in fact scarcely new. The 'realist' novel, as embodied in the work of Zola rather more than in that of Flaubert, had already been challenged by the experiments of James Joyce and Virginia Woolf which were known to her. Dostoevsky and Kafka, whom she (along with Sartre) much admired, appear as forerunners of fiction rooted in existential anguish. In France, among her immediate predecessors, neither André Gide with *Les Faux-Monnayeurs* nor André Malraux with *L'Espoir* could be said to write novels in the 'realist' mode, or novels where the representation of fully rounded characters in the nineteenth-century manner was predominant.

Simone de Beauvoir acknowledged the influence of contemporary American novelists — Ernest Hemingway, John Dos Passos, William Faulkner, Dashiell Hammett — upon her work. It consisted above all in matters of technique, with which she appeared to be preoccupied. She confessed to imitating in *Quand prime le spirituel* what she called 'the tone of false objectivity, of veiled irony' employed by Dos Passos in his trilogy *U.S.A.*[4] From Hemingway there came the concentration on seeing everything through one single consciousness, the rejection of 'supposedly objective descriptions' (all landscapes and objects being shown through the viewpoint of the protagonist and as a contribution to the action).[5] Hemingway's influence in this regard, she owned, was especially marked in *L'Invitée*, but his rule was one to which she remained faithful throughout her career as a novelist. From Faulkner she drew the handling of several subjective viewpoints, such as she was to follow in her own work. In the thrillers of Dashiell Hammett, she appreciated how each conversation had to reveal something new and contribute to the progress of the action. Moreover, it was largely through Hemingway that she chose to imitate the tone and rhythm of spoken language. Here she made a considerable contribution to the novel in France where a high literary tone had long prevailed.

For her contemporary French readers much of the originality of *L'Invitée*, which she began in 1937 under the title *Légitime Défense*, thus consisted in derivations from the American novel: in the absence of an omniscient narrator, the action being seen largely through the consciousness of Françoise, and to a lesser degree through Elisabeth and Gerbert; and in the striking use of the vernacular. In addition, the novel is sustained by ideas expressed in Sartre's *L'Etre et le Néant*, published in 1943 a few months before *L'Invitée* and dedicated to *Le Castor*. She herself had played no mean role in the preparation and development of this important philosophical work, through her discussions with him and her disagreement with some of his views. At first, Sartre had implied that everyone was totally free, whereas she had insisted that there were situations where freedom could not be exercised or where it was deceptive. He had ended by agreeing with her and had emphasised the importance of each human being's 'situation'. This stress on the individual's 'situation' or position in the world, a notion dear to Simone de Beauvoir — the concrete relationship with others and with circumstances at a given time — is central to *L'Invitée*. It helps to give a firm and distinct ideological framework to a story that, if stripped down to bare essentials, might simply appear as a fairly banal triangular relationship between Pierre and Françoise, a mature man and woman hitherto united, and Xavière, a young intruder.

For Simone de Beauvoir, as for Sartre, each individual consciousness can only grasp itself; it cannot see things through the consciousness of another. (Only the novelist can do that by means of inventing fictional personages.) 'I am *I* for myself

101

alone', she declared. Moreover, even this awareness has its limits. Another person (the Other) may have an entirely different image of one's appearance, personality and behaviour, an image that may radically contradict one's own sense of self. The awakening of Françoise to the fundamental hostility of Xavière's presence as the Other provides the dénouement of *L'Invitée*: 'This inimical presence which had just been revealed . . ., there was no longer any way of eluding the frightful unveiling of it . . . this unbridgeable obstacle . . . a foreign consciousness arose, free, absolute, relentless . . . Forever dispossessed of the world, Françoise herself melted away into an emptiness whose vague outline could not be seized by any word or image'.[7] The effect is shattering.

As for Pierre, he is surprised by the way this revelation has disturbed Françoise. Although he is an actor-manager like Charles Dullin, he sounds just like Sartre when he says:

It is quite true that each person experiences his own consciousness as an absolute. How could several absolutes prove compatible with each other? It is as mysterious as birth or death. It is even so knotty a problem that all philosophies come to grief over it. . . . What surprises me is that you should be upset by a metaphysical situation in so concrete a manner.[8]

Françoise explains to him that, for her (as for Simone de Beauvoir), an idea remains in the realm of theory until she herself actually experiences it. The reader cannot help hearing the voices of Sartre and Simone de Beauvoir in this fictional interchange.

Existential *Angst* — that sense of an abyss of nothingness underlying existence — can be set off by the root of a tree, as in Sartre's *La Nausée*, or by an article of clothing on an armchair, as in the example given by Simone de Beauvoir in *Mémoires d'une jeune fille rangée*. In her own experience, too, it could be aroused by the feeling that another person, like her friend Zaza or the actress Camille, sometimes eradicated her private sense of self. In *L'Invitée*, the dancer Paule makes Françoise feel 'like those faceless heads in the paintings of di Chirico'.[9]

In her long association with Pierre, Françoise has hitherto disregarded his infidelities. But now, after casually suggesting that she should take Xavière under her wing, he becomes obsessed with the girl, as he interprets her every expression and move (after the manner of Sartre with Olga). One of the striking aspects of this long novel is the immense richness of the study of minute variations and nuances of conduct and response drawn from so simple a *donnée* — the consequence, no doubt, of the subtle analyses of people that the companions liked to develop when they were teachers in Normandy. The threat that Xavière poses for Françoise (and for her so far stable association with Pierre) can only be removed by the elimination of the girl — a murder which the author significantly regarded as the motive force of the whole novel. It is literature as vengeance. Xavière herself, imperious, scornful, capricious, indifferent to the artistic standards and values by which Pierre and Françoise have lived, represents for her elders the mystery, attraction and dread aroused by a rebellious and free-living younger generation.

The 'situation' in which the characters find themselves is of major importance. Simone de Beauvoir later owned that, by transferring the trio from Rouen to Paris, she lost the stifling provincial ambience in which the original threesome of Sartre, Olga and herself had had its being. Yet the loss of verisimilitude is counterbalanced by the gain in cosmopolitan sophistication: the world of the theatre with its public dress-rehearsals attended by *le Tout-Paris*; the receptions in apartments decorated in the latest fashion with Japanese masks; the *bals nègres* and the cafés of Montparnasse and Saint-Germain-des-Prés, favoured by the intelligentsia of the 1930s. The Spanish Civil War, the Munich crisis, the threat of war — these overhang the private fluctuations of the trio. The posters for general mobilisation are pasted on the walls. Françoise sadly accompanies Pierre to the station when he is called up, just as Simone de Beauvoir watched Sartre's departure. The novel memorably evokes that oppressive and doomed world.

Neither Simone de Beauvoir nor Sartre spoke of the existentialist novel: she preferred to discuss 'the metaphysical novel', while he spoke of 'metaphysical writers'.[10] After the War, they both made public statements on this theme. Her essay 'Littérature et Métaphysique' was published in *Les Temps Modernes* in April 1946, before his essay 'Situation of the Writer in 1947' (a chapter in *Qu'est-ce que la littérature?*). Both of them made very similar remarks about the nature of the novel as they saw it then, similarities doubtless due to their private discussions over the years.

For Simone de Beauvoir, a novel serves as a journey of discovery for the reader as well as for the writer. It resembles a
quest, and not at all the systematic expression of philosophical or
psychological theories. No single meaning may be drawn from
such a novel. The 'metaphysical attitude' means 'establishing
oneself in one's totality vis-à-vis the totality of the world. Every
human event has a metaphysical significance beyond its psychological and social outlines since, through each of them, man is
wholly committed in the world as a whole; and doubtless there is
no one to whom this meaning has not been revealed at some
moment in his life'.[11] She refers here to the astonishment at one's
very being in existence that she had experienced as a girl and that
she gave to many of her fictional characters. According to her, it
is through joy, suffering, hope, revolt, that 'each man works out a
certain metaphysical situation which defines him much more
fundamentally than any of his psychological tendencies'.[12] The
'metaphysical viewpoint' is not narrower than any other, in her
opinion, because the psychological and social viewpoints can be
reconciled within it. This is her apologia.

A fictional character defined through his or her metaphysical
dimension — anguish, revolt, will-to-power, fear of death, evasion,
thirst for the absolute — need not be more of a fabrication (in her
view) than a miser or a coward who is characterised by his
psychological traits (say, in the manner of Balzac). The models
to whom she alludes and with whom she concurs are Dostoevsky
and Kafka, without apparently perceiving how much they both
owe to the solidity of Dickens, and how concentrated is their
passionate intensity. The metaphysical novel seems to her to be
the most accomplished variety in the genre because it brings 'an
unveiling of existence', because it tries to grasp man and events in
their relationship to 'the totality of the world', and because it can
conjure up human destiny in all its 'living ambiguity'.[13]

This element of ambiguity is clearly essential to her understanding of the novel. Why does Françoise choose to kill Xavière?
Because she is jealous of the girl's youth and power, or because
the intruder, by her aggressive attitudes, reveals the falsity and
the shortcomings of Françoise's idealised association with Pierre
and therefore of her whole mode of life? Or is it because the older
woman has taken the young actor Gerbert from Xavière and

cannot bear the way in which this betrayal undermines her own sense of the kind of person she always thought she was? A number of interpretations might be adduced for Françoise's act, which remains partly 'out of character' and partly an enduring puzzle, in the manner of life itself.

Simone de Beauvoir followed Kierkegaard (and Sartre) in defining existentialism as a philosophy of ambiguity in her essay, 'Pour une Morale de l'ambiguïté'. There, she spoke of 'the ambiguity of our condition' — according to Sartre, the human condition is ambiguous because man is both being and not-being, body and consciousness. For her, on no account was 'ambiguity' to be confused with 'absurdity' — the concept expressed through André Malraux's *Les Conquérants* or *La Condition humaine*, or through *L'Etranger* and other writings of Albert Camus. In Simone de Beauvoir's understanding, 'the absurd' signifies that life cannot be given a meaning, whereas 'the ambiguous' implies that the meaning of life has to be won (or rather, that each person has to strive to attain it). In her opinion, therefore, existentialist ambiguity rejects the pessimism that is all-too-often associated with it.

The artist, for Simone de Beauvoir, has to be 'placed' or 'in situation' in the world. As she sees it, the psychological novelist studies the human heart in general; he is not concerned with 'the situation' of his protagonist. Here, he differs from the existential or metaphysical novelist who rejects the very idea of 'human nature' (since, after Sartre, being precedes essence). The notion of such a constant as 'human nature' to which we all conform is regarded as a trap to prevent people from trying to do anything to improve the condition of their fellow-creatures. That is the drift of Simone de Beauvoir's very partial attack on her 'bourgeois' literary contemporaries in her essay, 'La Pensée de droite, aujourd'hui'. However, she saw her essays and her novels as serving entirely different functions.

The essay, expressing one particular attitude, should present this attitude as strongly as possible, and should 'provoke' the reader. On the other hand, the novel should not express one single idea, nor should it reach a clear-cut conclusion that can be paraphrased or summed up in a few words. The novel, unlike the essay, should reveal the ambiguity of experience: that is why (she said) she disliked fiction that introduced real people under fictitious names (*roman à clef*), or fiction that proposed or expounded a thesis (*roman à thèse*). Since she would be accused — with some justification — of writing both, it is not surprising that she fiercely defended herself. Certainly, it was not really her intention to write *romans à clef* or *romans à thèse*, but her want of inventive powers sometimes led her into doing so.

After her labours on *L'Invitée*, Simone de Beauvoir dreamed of writing 'vast committed novels'.[14] What she actually wrote emerged as two novels on moral and metaphysical themes whose socio-political aspects ultimately appear subordinate. Both *Le Sang des autres* (1945) and to a greater degree *Tous les Hommes sont mortels* (1946) represented a sustained effort to move beyond her own literal experiences. With *Le Sang des autres* she required some knowledge of the labour movements of the 1930s, and of the Resistance, with which she had little connection. *Tous les Hommes sont mortels* was constructed upon a huge historical canvas: it ranged from medieval Italy to the Spain of the Emperor Charles V and his possessions in the New World; and from eighteenth-century France with its ideas of progress and enlightenment to the abortive revolution of 1832 and the Revolution of February 1848; the whole being framed by a prologue and epilogue set in the present day. Although *Le Sang des autres* was well received in 1945, possibly in part because of the discussion of moral dilemmas arising from actions in the Resistance movement, neither of these novels succeeded in attracting a lasting public in the same way as *L'Invitée* or the later *Les Mandarins*, for reasons that eventually became clear to the author. They are not 'ambiguous' in their effect: they reach a single conclusion and are overly moralistic and didactic.

The epigraph of *Le Sang des autres* is taken from Dostoevsky: 'Each person is responsible for everything in the face of everyone'. These words are repeated by the protagonist, Jean Blomart, who remarks: 'That seems so very true to me'.[15] It is a shattering observation, suggesting that each individual bears responsibility for all the evil as well as all the good in the world, and it is clearly one to which the author herself grew to adhere. Like many a hero of left-wing novels of the 1930s, Blomart, though born into the bourgeoisie, becomes so moved by the plight of the underprivileged that he throws in his lot with the workers. His friend, the apolitical artist Marcel (modelled on the sculptor Giacometti), rightly notes that '[there] will always be a gulf between a worker and yourself: you choose freely a condition to which he is subject'.[16] Blomart, having led Marcel's brother, the young poet Jacques, to join the Communist Party, cannot overcome his guilt when Jacques is killed. Leaving the Party, Blomart engages in the labour movement, but whatever he does he is haunted by 'the crime of existence' — surely an echo of the doctrine of original sin which the author had ostensibly rejected long before.[17]

Blomart's refusal to commit himself to the egocentric, apolitical Hélène, who loves him, proves deeply damaging to her. Ultimately, though noted for indifference, Hélène awakens to a sense of responsibility when she witnesses the fate of the Jews. So she chooses to be sent on a dangerous mission after joining Blomart's Resistance organisation, a mission during which she is fatally wounded. Events are seen partly through a series of complex flashbacks as Blomart watches at the dying Hélène's bedside. 'The blood of others and our own is the same', says the Communist Paul.[18] The book closes with Blomart's realisation that he will never escape 'the curse of existence'; but suffering will not have been in vain while he defends freedom, 'that supreme good'. He has found 'the courage ever to accept risk and anguish, to bear my crimes and the remorse that will endlessly tear at my vitals. There is no other way'.[19] It is a conclusion well suited to the spirit of the time in France — the book having been undertaken in 1941 and completed in 1943.

The powerful central 'metaphysical' themes of the novel — the pain of being unable to save others, the responsibility of the individual for his abstention as well as for his choices and his deeds, the attempt to find a counterbalance to the ineluctable sense of futility — are undermined by the contrivances of the plot and the failure of the characters to come to life. They are like walking moral dilemmas. And this despite the fact that the author has given them some of her own experiences, like the visit she paid to Sartre in the army at Brumath in 1939, and the exodus from Paris in June 1940 in which she participated.

A similar criticism of lifelessness might be levelled at *Tous les Hommes sont mortels*, not surprisingly, since one of the principal characters, Fosca, born in thirteenth-century Carmona, has drunk the 'elixir of immortality'. Whatever the variety of historical background against which he is projected, and whatever his aims, the fact that he cannot die transforms him into a non-human figure; so that it may seem rather perverse to compose a large volume to demonstrate that 'all men are mortal', and that their very humanity resides in their mortality.

Fosca begins with an urge to achieve the good of his city, Carmona, and then the good of Italy as a whole. His acts, despite their virtuous aim, are marked by ever-increasing ruthlessness. As confidential adviser to the Emperor Charles V, he believes that at last he has the opportunity to improve the entire world, and that he will be able to create an earthly paradise. 'Do you think that you can ever do good in this world without doing evil?', Fosca asks the Emperor.[20] There follow dreadful massacres — the hideous 'mechanism' that is at work throughout the centuries to frustrate human happiness and the yearning for a just and rational society. All effort seems useless: one can do nothing for others, admits Fosca. The Emperor agrees, and abdicates. Régine, the vain and ambitious actress who has discovered Fosca's secret, and to whom he is relating his tale in the present day, begs him: 'Do not go on; it is a waste of time. It will be the same story right to the end, I know it'.[21] That is a risky thing to make a fictional character say at the end of Part 2, when there are three more parts and an epilogue to follow.

Inevitably, Fosca's human bonds turn to ashes as soon as his offspring, or his new friend, or his new beloved, realises he or she must die while Fosca himself will survive. The fable reaches its climax when he witnesses the heroic resistance in the cloître Saint-Merri during the abortive attempt at revolution in 1832. It is curious that Simone de Beauvoir should choose as the culminating episode of her fable the same failed revolution that inspired Victor Hugo's account of the barricades in *Les Misérables*. A 'successful' revolution is all-too-often followed by the corruption of the ideal, whereas an unsuccessful one still carries with it an aura of heroic sacrifice and the hope of better things to come. Certainly, the space allotted to the revolutionary triumph of February 1848 in Simone de Beauvoir's novel is brief.

The revolutionary retains his faith, whatever the outcome: 'For me, it is a great thing to be a man', says Garnier, and to feel himself a man among men.[22] He can choose his death, after the manner of Katow who sacrifices himself for others at the end of

Malraux's *La Condition humaine*. The immortal Fosca realises that '[these] were men who wished to fulfil their human destiny by choosing their life and their death: they were free men'.[23] During the Revolution of 1848 with which his tale ends, he understands that, unlike his companions, he is not truly alive because he cannot risk his life in the struggle as they have done: 'They were men, they were living. I myself was not one of them. I had nothing to hope for'.[24] The stress on free will by the revolutionaries does little to remove the final depressing effect of this long meditation on life, time and death, which concludes with Régine's overpowering horror at her own mortality. Action is willed, whereas the fear is deeply felt.

What is the use? ('A quoi bon?'). That is the query which underlies a great deal of Simone de Beauvoir's work. The dread of death, of nothingness or 'the vertiginous void', the lasting awareness of the vanity of vanities — all this is subsumed under the heading of what she calls 'the point of view of Sirius', the Dogstar.[25] All the same, she attacked any writer who sought to adopt the lofty standpoint of eternity in contemplating human affairs, because she saw it as an alibi for doing nothing. One of her main targets in this regard was Henry de Montherlant, proponent of acceptance and abstention. How closely she remained secretly attuned to his destructive rhetoric, though, can be seen in her injunction that one must 'keep oneself above the void'[26] — surely an unconscious allusion to the last line of his celebrated essay, 'Chevalerie du Néant' in his *Service inutile*.

This all-pervading sense of *vanitas* is counterbalanced by the determined affirmation of life values, through stress on working with and for one's fellow-creatures, however dangerously and tragically this may be linked with violence — the 'mechanism' of ruthlessness that figures in both *Le Sang des autres* and *Tous les Hommes sont mortels*. The novels give expression to the view of Cinéas in her essay, 'Pyrrhus et Cinéas' (published in 1944): '"What is the use?" he says; and he goes on with his task . . .'.[27] These words may also be regarded as the central moral position of her most forceful novel, *Les Mandarins*.

Here, the author is concerned to present the moral dilemmas of a number of French intellectuals in the immediate postwar period.

The 'metaphysical situation' is revealed through two viewpoints: the consciousness of Anne, a psychiatrist and wife of the important writer, Robert Dubreuilh, or that of their friend, the novelist Henri Perron. Both Dubreuilh and Perron are engaged in political journalism just like Sartre and Camus, and there is also an attempt to promote the SRL, a third force similar to the RDR in which Sartre was involved for a time. Events that actually occurred some years later (like the controversy over the existence of labour camps in the Soviet Union), are moved back to the period 1945–7. The upsurge of hope that accompanies the Liberation soon fades in the horror of the hydrogen bomb, the persistence of world hunger, the hostilities of the cold war. Ideals become eroded or corrupted, friendships disintegrate, in the general messiness of life. The leading French intellectuals who issued from the Resistance thinking that they had won influence to change the world for the better, gradually realise that France is no longer a world power and that they are as impotent as the Chinese mandarins to whom the title alludes. The theme of powerlessness and futility therefore contradicts the element of action.

Simone de Beauvoir liked to insist that *Les Mandarins* was not a *roman à clef*, and certainly she did not want it to appear to be one. Yet there are obvious similarities between the fictional characters and real persons: Scriassine, as we have already noted, invites memories of Arthur Koestler; while Lewis Brogan occupies a similar place in Anne's life to that of Nelson Algren in the author's, however truncated the love affair in the novel. Such characters are barely disguised: they are not moulded of elements taken from various sources, as is usual in the creation of fictional figures. Anne may not be a writer, but she is given many of her creator's responses, and she stands *vis-à-vis* her complaisant husband Robert, portrayed as many years older than his model, Sartre, in a union similar to that of the companions where physical relations no longer play a part. Their daughter, the selfish, amoral and difficult Nadine, clearly has something in common with the author's recalcitrant protégées. Simone de Beauvoir admitted in *La Force des choses* that she was taking revenge through Nadine on 'Lise' (Nathalie Sorokine) and other young women for their sexual aggressiveness.

As for the novelist Henri Perron, he is endowed with many of his creator's views on literature, and his connection with Camus is rather less evident than has been supposed. All the same, Simone de Beauvoir's resentment at Camus's lofty public moral stance, which she considered to be at odds with his private life, permeates her depiction of Henri. Thus, because of his liaison with the actress Josette — who becomes subject to blackmail along with her mother on account of their association with the Nazis during the Occupation — Henri gives false testimony against two survivors, in a scene of grim and painful irony.

There are limits to any direct or oblique parallels, of course, and the fun to be derived from them. *Les Mandarins* would not be the important novel it still remains, and Simone de Beauvoir's most valuable contribution to the genre, if it were nothing more than a *roman à clef*. It is certainly her most ambitious and wide-ranging novel, one into which she poured so much of herself and her own experience that she never again attempted anything like it on a similar scale. The value of the book lies not in any strict factual accuracy but rather in the evocation of a particular ambience, with its soul-searching, its guilt complexes, its 'ambiguous' responses. It is still a 'metaphysical' novel, concerned with 'situation', consciousness, existential *Angst*, though less obviously so than its immediate predecessors. Indeed, *Les Mandarins* even contains a blueprint of the author's artistic intentions in Henri's concept of the novel he wishes to write: 'Why not undertake a novel that concerns a date and a situation, one which would mean something? Tell a story of today where readers would find their own cares and problems. Neither to prove anything nor to preach, but to bear witness', muses Henri.[28]

In one of its facets *Les Mandarins* is also a thriller of sorts, where those who collaborated with the Nazis are still being pursued by avenging individuals like Vincent, who cannot bear to see any *salaud* escape punishment. Notwithstanding Simone de Beauvoir's approval of the *épuration*, in 'Œil pour œil' and in her autobiography, she has Henri strongly object to it when he discovers that Vincent is involved in the self-appointed assassination gangs. The death of Lambert's father, a suspected collaborator, is thought to be no accident. Despite his earlier objections, however, Henri later helps Vincent to conceal the body of a drug-addict who betrayed innocent people to the Gestapo. In this manner, Simone de Beauvoir manages indirectly to convey her own views, together with the objections to those views, and this method is employed throughout the book.

Another facet of the novel concerns various types of love. One is the extravagantly idealised love of the one-time singer Paule who has given up her career for Henri (a false passion modelled on the crazed infatuation of Renée Ballon for Malraux in some of its details), although it is obvious to all and even to herself that her lover has tired of her. Attracted to the beautiful, vain young actress, Josette, who appears in his new play, Henri drifts into a liaison with her. Finally, he settles down in marriage with the unpredictable Nadine.

As for Anne, approaching forty, and attending a conference of psychiatrists in the USA, she seeks an adventure in Chicago with the American novelist, Lewis Brogan, which develops on both sides into an intensely passionate love affair. Yet Anne's refusal to commit herself totally to Lewis (so named after the egotistical composer, Lewis Dodd, in *The Constant Nymph*?) arouses his resentment, just as the author's refusal of marriage inspired Nelson Algren's. There is an accomplished scene when Anne and Lewis return to New York from Mexico: she believes that he has been as rapturously happy as herself, while he — much to her surprise — lets her know that he thinks she takes more than she gives. The different expectations of the sexes are subtly revealed through vivid dialogue. Lewis grows ever more moody and self-centred in his angry disappointment with Anne — a portrait of the American writer that obliquely suggests the author's resentment at Algren's behaviour towards herself on her last visit to Chicago, and goes some way to explain his later violent outbursts.

As regards the political facet of the book, this concerns the whole question of the value of Leftist commitment and involvement in 'action' on the part of French literary intellectuals. These figures are studied in a particular 'situation', the period immediately following the victory of the Resistance movement, the euphoric hour of Liberation, the very moment when Sartre had proclaimed the superior worth of *littérature engagée*. The relation between literature and politics is discussed at various points in the novel. The anti-Stalinist Scriassine envisages the likelihood of literature being swallowed up by politics; and a debate follows about whether the former takes precedence over the latter. The eminent writer, anti-Fascist and Resistance hero, Robert Dubreuilh, declares that the revolution must come first. Anne, his former pupil, now his wife, fears lest he may join the Communists one day, despite his criticism of them. Then he would have to follow the Party line, and she considers that to do so would be harmful to his work. Here can be heard an echo of Simone de Beauvoir's private doubts, given to a fictional character who is not a writer but who keenly values her husband's *œuvre*.

Dubreuilh appears as the person most zealous in his commitment to left-wing politics and to the Soviet Union. It is he who persuades Henri (rather against that novelist's will) to bring his paper into service with the third force. As detailed information about the Soviet labour camps begins to percolate, Robert is opposed to publishing it (unlike Sartre who, according to Simone de Beauvoir, did so at once). Through Robert's opposition and Henri's indecision, the author is able to polarise the dispute between publishing or withholding the truth. Anne expresses the humanist view that an intellectual has a moral obligation to tell the truth. For Robert, however, the old values of truth, liberty and individual morality have to be 'reinvented'; in the face of world hunger, humanism and individualism are 'vile'; and besides, 'my duties as an intellectual, respect for the truth, are stuff and nonsense', he roundly declares.[29] He rejects received morality in the name of some 'new' morality that will settle for lies in order to preserve hope and protect the cause. On the other hand, Henri feels that he must publish the truth about the Soviet labour camps. The pussyfooting editorial that he composes none the less prompts Dubreuilh to break with him.

The whole fracas, therefore, seems to be less about the actual suffering of the people in the labour camps, or about any desire to help them by telling their story, than about the moral obligations of the intellectual, and whether or not he should be faithful to the truth as he understands it. At first it may appear that the author holds the balance between the hitherto accepted view of intellectual integrity and the so-called 'new' morality (or rather amorality), sponsored by Dubreuilh who — like Sartre — comes to condemn literature and to allot an ever larger role to violence and terror. But this is not the case. For Henri is as much of a fellow-traveller as Dubreuilh, only he is more wishy-washy. When the two men are reconciled (unlike Sartre and Camus), it is plain that Henri has always chosen the Soviet Union against the United States. Anne, like Henri, may voice doubts, but significantly she ends in agreement with her husband. The debate is thus weighted in favour of saving the face of the Stalinist regime, and in this respect the novel, while it skilfully eludes the more obvious pitfalls of agitprop, cannot fail to appear in part as a *roman à thèse*. The attempt to restore some degree of 'ambiguity' in the final chapter, through Anne's return to themes of existential anguish and questioning, does not entirely serve to erase this impression.

In the years that followed, Simone de Beauvoir published only one relatively short novel, *Les Belles Images* (1966), dedicated to Claude Lanzmann. It is perhaps her most accomplished work of fiction in the formal sense: there is one dominant theme, and everything contributes to it. All is seen through Laurence, whose career lies in advertising (or the selling of beautiful images). Apparently happily married, she lives the outwardly successful life of well-to-do professional people, whose status is defined by their possessions and by their modish habits and opinions. The book offers a sustained criticism of the world of 'beautiful images', of the technocratic or 'consumer' society (soon to be an object of attack during the *événements* of May 1968); and it elaborates the author's long-standing detestation of the bourgeoisie and its ways.

Complacency is soon shattered: Laurence's young daughter Catherine is disturbed by what she has heard from Brigitte, a slightly older Jewish friend, who has communicated to the child something of her own awareness of suffering. The reaction of Catherine tears through the veil that is obscuring Laurence's vision of life. The suffering of others impinges on Laurence as it does so often on Simone de Beauvoir's fictional characters to stimulate a development or a reversal. (While she was working on this novel, she composed a preface to Jean-François Steiner's book on the agony of the Jews in the notorious extermination camp, *Treblinka*. It was in this preface that she endorsed his stress on Jewish resistance to the Nazis.)

Laurence's husband, Jean-Charles, and members of her family are prepared to break up the association between the two young girls. Even her own father, whom Laurence has loved and much admired for his cultivation and apparent wisdom, is found wanting where the response to human suffering is concerned. Laurence suffers a nervous breakdown: she believes it is too late for herself, but she wants Catherine to have the chance to attain authenticity. And so she stands up to her husband by insisting that the girl's friendship with Brigitte should be allowed to continue. Skilfully and smoothly constructed as it is, the novel seems thin and the plot mechanism artificial. All is weighted against the majority of the members of Laurence's circle, and the battle seems won in advance.

Simone de Beauvoir's last published fictional work consisted of three short stories, known by the title of the most effective of them, 'La Femme rompue' (1968). They are studies of women in advancing years, written just before she began her sociological and cultural enquiry into old age, *La Vieillesse* (published in 1970). The women in her tales have to confront the ravages of time as well as the pain of change and loneliness. The last words of the abandoned wife in 'La Femme rompue' are 'I am afraid'.[30] None of these stories can be called tonic. They uncover women's self-deception, their resentment against men, their folly in not assuring their own independence, and their despair when they are left with nothing but the prospect of lonely decline and death.

The metaphysical novel as advocated by Simone de Beauvoir lays stress on response to 'situation' (a person's sex, social class, the historic circumstances of the era) and on existential anguish. Ideals and aspirations all too often end in disillusion. The passing of time, the differing expectations and reactions of the sexes, the dread of age and loneliness, the terror of death and nothingness — these recur in her fiction, and they become more insistent. A kind of Kafkaesque horror at human existence underlies her work, a horror that is challenged by her intense passion for life but is never really vanquished by it.

The repetition of the same varieties of existential *Angst* in her novels and stories makes for a certain monotony. It is not so much the transposition of autobiographical elements into fiction, a procedure common to most novelists in varying degrees, but the way in which her fictional characters are given, say, her own inexplicable rages as a child, her sudden loss of religious faith, her pleasure in taking risks by mountain climbing alone, and so forth.

These details from her own life presumably help to give solid body to fictional personages who are not being presented in a traditional or 'realist' way, since she has rejected the 'realist' mode in the novel.

When discussing her fiction in her autobiographical works, Simone de Beauvoir concentrates to a great extent on matters of technique, especially the question of 'point of view'. Her self-criticism gives an impression of honesty, but it also serves to direct the reader's attention to the place she wishes it to go. Perhaps she had learned this strategy from a master at it: Henry de Montherlant in his extensive prefaces and postfaces to his plays. Her own remarks reveal how she wanted her books to be read, not necessarily how they should be read.

Throughout her life she defended the metaphysical novel, chiefly by attacking (in her autobiography, her articles and lectures, and even in *Les Belles Images*) the proponents of the *nouveau roman*, particularly Nathalie Sarraute, and to a lesser degree Alain Robbe-Grillet and Michel Butor. She disliked what she called the old French obsession with psychology, the concern with the look of things. She found them boring: ' . . . they turn their backs on human beings', she complained.[31] What is more, everything to do with politics is left out of their work. This deliberate omission of political commitment on the part of adherents of the *nouveau roman* naturally offended her since it challenged her own writings.

Yet Simone de Beauvoir is not strictly a political novelist, despite her apparent concern with political matters in *Le Sang des autres* or *Les Mandarins*. When she falls into the kind of *littérature de gauche*[32] or Leftist literature to which Robert Dubreuilh aspires in *Les Mandarins* she betrays her own ideal of 'living ambiguity'. Primarily, she is concerned with dilemmas of existence and of moral conduct and social responsibility to which there is no single answer. It is here that her relentless probing, her blend of simplicity and lyricism are at their best. Although it provided an ideological framework, the concept of the metaphysical novel was perhaps a constricting one. After all, Sartre did not finish *Les Chemins de la liberté* and gave up writing fiction; while Simone de Beauvoir's novelistic dynamism ultimately petered out, to be replaced by journalism, social studies and autobiographical works.

Notes

1. *La Force de l'âge*, p. 107.
2. *Quand prime le spirituel*, Gallimard, 1979, pp. 9–10.
3. Ibid., pp. 248–9.
4. *La Force de l'âge*, p. 230.
5. Ibid., p. 353; see also pp. 144–5.
6. 'Mon Expérience d'écrivain' (1966), in *Les Ecrits de Simone de Beauvoir*, p. 456.
7. *L'Invitée*, p. 318.
8. Ibid., p. 329.
9. Ibid. (1948 edn), p. 289.
10. 'Littérature et Métaphysique', in *L'Existentialisme et la sagesse des nations*, p. 106; Sartre, *Qu'est-ce que la littérature?* (1948), Collection Idées, Gallimard, 1966, p. 268.
11. 'Littérature et Métaphysique', p. 99.
12. Ibid., pp. 99–100.
13. Ibid., pp. 106–7.
14. *La Force de l'âge*, p. 570.
15. *Le Sang des autres*, p. 114.
16. Ibid., p. 26.
17. Ibid., p. 25.
18. Ibid., p. 123.
19. Ibid., p. 224.
20. *Tous les Hommes sont mortels* (1946), Gallimard, 1947, p. 171.
21. Ibid., p. 216.
22. Ibid., p. 326.
23. Ibid., p. 327.
24. Ibid., p. 353.
25. *La Force des choses*, p. 75.
26. Interview with Caroline Moorehead (2), *The Times*, 16 May 1974.
27. *Pyrrhus et Cinéas* (with 'Pour une Morale de l'ambiguïté'), Collection Idées, 1974, p. 369.
28. *Les Mandarins* (1954), Folio Gallimard, 1972, vol. 1, p. 426.
29. Ibid., vol. 1, pp. 278–9, 372; vol. 2, p. 69.
30. *La Femme rompue*, Gallimard, 1968, p. 251.
31. *La Force des choses*, p. 649.
32. *Les Mandarins*, 1, p. 376.

8 The Marble of the Ages

What remains of Simone de Beauvoir's activity and work? She herself uttered disclaimers about wishing to survive for posterity. These serve as a kind of insurance: people deny that they want something they feel they may not obtain. Often such denials were accompanied by a little proviso. 'I did not aspire to the marble of the ages', she declared, while admitting that she would not have been satisfied with small acclaim.[1] She owned that with *La Force de l'âge* and *La Force des choses* she was not aiming to create 'a work of art', a term which seemed to her to have the boring frigidity of garden statuary, and to be one for collectors rather than creators.[2] Where her literary work was concerned, she wanted (just like George Sand) to make an impact by being read by a great many people while she was still alive. As for posterity, she did not 'give a damn' — remembering to add 'or almost'.[3] This cavalier or modest-seeming attitude may be taken with a pinch of salt. A record is penned in order to leave a mark in history.

Where blood (or consideration for the feelings of others) is so often sacrificed to ink, it may be assumed that literature is being taken very seriously indeed, despite the modish devaluation of long-treasured cultural values in favour of revolutionary and utopian socialist ideals. There is a moment in *Les Mandarins* when Nadine complains bitterly that Henri has used her very own words in his novel and that this is 'a breach of trust'.[4] Henri brushes this aside with a certain condescension. Wanda Kosakiewicz was so outraged by the novel that she thrust a kitchen knife through a copy of *Les Mandarins*, cut her wrist, and nearly died.[5] Her sister Olga was deeply upset when Simone de Beauvoir published Sartre's letters, with their unflattering allusions to herself, and she refused to have anything more to do with her. The writer speaks about 'transposition' in fiction, the method of passing beyond what she calls 'anecdote' (or the actual circumstances of the *donnée*).[6] This process depends upon the skill and tact of the novelist. More would appear to be at stake than mere transposition.

It seems that Simone de Beauvoir sometimes regarded literature as both personal and general therapy. In theory, to tell it as it is means to help reader as well as writer, though the portrayal of her mother's humiliation during her fatal illness and of Sartre's incontinence and other physical weaknesses in clinical detail might be regarded as 'a breach of trust'. Clearly, ink takes precedence, and there is an element of coldness and even to some extent a settling of scores. Literature for her is a form of catharsis, even a way of getting rid of bad feeling, whether irritation or grudge. Her accounts of the death of Jacques, of Camille, of 'Lise', bear witness to this strain in the autobiography. In fiction it may be traced not only in the murder of Xavière, but to some degree in the treatment of Pierre, a shadowy figure in *L'Invitée* but also one who inspires resentment and momentary hatred. Often husbands and lovers in Simone de Beauvoir's fiction are viewed with similar direct or oblique ill-will (Lewis in *Les Mandarins*, Jean-Charles in *Les Belles Images*, or Maurice in 'La Femme rompue').

As a writer, Simone de Beauvoir can be obsessed with herself, in small matters and large. She records the trivia of her existence as well as the important contacts and events. When she writes of Charles Dullin's death in *La Vieillesse*, it is 'an entire section of my own life that crumbled away'.[7] A similar reference to self is frequently made when she alludes to the death of friends.

The charge of egocentricity may be counterbalanced by her many acts of generosity: her unstinting assistance to 'prentice writers like the actor Marcel Mouloudji or Violette Leduc; her defence of victims of torture, such as the young Algerian woman, Djamila Boupacha; her writings on behalf of underprivileged women or the aged poor. She knew perfectly well how little her signature on manifestos achieved, though she felt it was impossible not to sign, so long as such interventions were occasionally effective in saving lives or obtaining the release of prisoners of conscience.

Throughout the autobiography, there runs an account of her reactions to political affairs in which others were actively engaged: her anxiety, her indignation, her anger, her tears, her pain and horror at the suffering of the victims, her disaffection, even her 'satisfaction' at the humiliating French defeat at Dien Bien Phu which ended the war in Indochina. This emotional response, accompanied by a disinclination to participate in the political process of French democracy, gives constant proof of her sense of her right feelings while freeing her from responsibility in any decisions that are taken.

For her, as for Sartre, the main task of the intellectual is unfailingly to challenge authority — and that is why she considered André Malraux quite wrong to have become Gaullist Minister of Culture. The assumption is that authority can never be right — at least if it is the authority of one's own country. This stance of sustained opposition can even lead to gratification at her country's defeat. Such intellectual hatred of her culture and civilisation while at the same time serving it through her literary efforts is difficult to appreciate. It is a type of alienation that has grown more common.

The total freedom, sincerity and authenticity exalted by Sartrian existentialism appear as a mirage. Nowhere is this more evident than in personal relationships. There may well be shortcomings in the institution of marriage, but it is equally plain that there are shortcomings also in any other type of union. Since human beings are involved, there are going to be limitations on perfection. To have exorbitant expectations is to court disappointment and disillusion. The part played by self-deception in her novels is extensive, and it is not confined to the obvious self-deceivers like Elisabeth in *L'Invitée* or Paule in *Les Mandarins*: it is revealed also through those who otherwise pride themselves on their lucidity.

Similar exorbitant expectations are betrayed by her social and political utterances. These are fuelled by a passionate desire, after Marx, to change man and to change life. Her study of old age offers an important exposé of current abuses and it brings a hitherto largely neglected theme before the general public. Yet it is marred by extremism. Asking rhetorically how far society is responsible for an individual's decline, she can say that the age when senility begins depends on class, ignoring the possibility of disease or act of God. In an ideal society, she maintains, old age would scarcely exist. Though herself in her sixties at the time of writing, she still has the notion beloved of youth that an ideal society is capable of realisation: 'Old age proclaims the failure of our entire civilisation. It is man as a whole who must be recast, all the relationships between men that must be recreated. . . . The whole system is at stake and the demand can only be a radical one: to change life'.[8] Her rejection of improvements in the

120

areas she discussed, in favour of overthrow and an impossible ideal, stayed constant in her writings almost to the last as a token of immaturity. It is one of the factors that mars also her travel books on the United States and China, both of which have faded into an obscurity where they are likely to remain.

As for *Le Deuxième Sexe*, it has already acquired the status of an historical landmark. Its contribution to the awakening and advancement of women can scarcely be denied. For some women writers, Simone de Beauvoir has become a symbol, or symbolic mother, as one has it, a person with whom they engage in dialogue in a quest for their own identity. She looked further than equality (which has yet to be realised) towards total sexual freedom, without apparently perceiving that here, as elsewhere in the social and political realm, human beings have to pay a price for every advance.

Unlike her predecessor, Mme de Staël, Simone de Beauvoir made no contribution to political thought as such. Rather her influence is to be found in the field of social questions where she had the talent to provoke controversy and reflection. Her autobiography, in all its volumes, will stand as an invaluable document to be consulted — along with *Les Mandarins* — for the manners and conduct, entertainments and travels, beliefs and ideals, illusions and self-delusions of one influential sector of the French intelligentsia with its international ramifications.

The funeral of Simone de Beauvoir in April 1986 was a much quieter affair than that of Sartre, whose body was followed to the Montparnasse cemetery by a vast mass of people. In her grief at the time of his death in hospital, she had tried to lie down under the sheet with his corpse. A nurse dissuaded her, because gangrene had already set in. Instead, she lay down on top of the sheet. In this act of high melodrama, she made one of the last of her attempts to claim him. Even in death he contrived to evade her total control and her desire to impose upon posterity the image of an ideal union, just as he had in life.

Notes

1. *La Force de l'âge*, p. 577.
2. *La Force des choses*, p. 8.

3. Ibid., p. 58.
4. *Les Mandarins*, 2, pp. 459–60.
5. Letter to Nelson Algren, quoted in C. Francis and F. Gontier, *Simone de Beauvoir*, pp. 289–90; see also p. 388.
6. *La Force de l'âge*, p. 109.
7. *La Vieillesse*, Gallimard, 1970, p. 389.
8. Ibid., pp. 569–70.

Chronology

1905	21 June	Jean-Paul Sartre born.
1906		Captain Dreyfus rehabilitated.
1908	9 January	Simone de Beauvoir born.
1913		She attends the Cours Désir.
1914		France at war with Germany.
1917	October	Bolsheviks seize power in Russia.
1918	November	Armistice.
1920		French Communist Party founded at Tours.
1922	October	Mussolini's blackshirts march on Rome.
1925–6		She studies at Institut Catholique and at Institut Sainte-Marie de Neuilly; joins Catholic association for workers' education led by Robert Garric.
1928		Works for *agrégation* in philosophy at Ecole Normale Supérieure as well as for her degree (*licence-ès-lettres*) at the Sorbonne.
1929		Through René Maheu ('André Herbaud') she meets Jean-Paul Sartre at the Ecole Normale Supérieure. Sartre proposes a two-year agreement; he continues his association with Simone-Camille Sans (Camille). Death of her schoolfriend, Zaza.
1931		She obtains teaching post at Marseilles.
	Summer	She visits Spain with Sartre.
1932		She moves to *lycée* in Rouen.

1933	January	Hitler becomes Chancellor.
		Sartre and Simone de Beauvoir form a 'trio' with Olga Kosakiewicz.
	September	Sartre studies at Institut Français in Berlin where he becomes attached to 'Marie Girard'.
1934	Feb. and July/Aug.	Simone de Beauvoir visits Sartre twice in Berlin.
1935		She begins the book later known as *Quand prime le spirituel*.
1936	3 May	Popular Front government in France.
	Summer	She visits Italy with Sartre.
	18 July	Spanish Civil War breaks out.
		She teaches at lycée Molière in Paris.
1937		Collapse of the 'trio' with Olga Kosakiewicz.
	January	Moscow show trials begin.
		She falls seriously ill with pneumonia; convalesces in the South of France: liaison with Jacques-Laurent Bost.
	Summer	She visits Greece with Sartre and Jacques-Laurent Bost. She begins *Légitime Défense* (afterwards known as *L'Invitée*).
1938	29 September	France and Britain sign Munich Agreement with Hitler.
1939	15–16 March	The Germans occupy Czechoslovakia.
	28 March	End of Spanish Civil War: victory of General Franco.
	End July	Sartre's liaison with Wanda Kosakiewicz.
	23 August	Nazi–Soviet non-aggression pact signed.
	1 September	Germans invade Poland.
	2 September	Sartre is called up.
	3 September	War declared.
1940	10 May	German blitzkrieg through France.
	10 June	She joins exodus from Paris.
	14 June	The Germans enter Paris.

	18 June	General de Gaulle broadcasts from London to the French nation.
	21 June	Sartre taken prisoner.
	22 June	Marshal Pétain signs armistice with Germany.
	28 June	She returns to occupied Paris; resumes her teaching post; signs document that she is neither a Freemason nor a Jew.
1941	March	Sartre returns from Stalag XII D.
	Spring	The resistance group 'Socialisme et Liberté' is founded by Sartre and others to disseminate information; it is abandoned in October.
	22 June	Hitler invades USSR; the French Communists now support the resistance movement.
	Summer	Sartre and Simone de Beauvoir on cycling tour of South of France.
	8 July	Death of Simone de Beauvoir's father.
	7 December	The Japanese attack Pearl Harbor. The United States enters the war.
1942–3		She works on *Le Sang des autres*
1942	16 July	The great round-up (*la grande rafle*): Jews, including children, deported to concentration camps and death camps.
1943	January	Sartre becomes a member of the Communist-front Comité National des Ecrivains. She is dismissed from her teaching post for her influence over her pupil, Nathalie Sorokine ('Lise'); she works for Radio Vichy.
	August	*L'Invitée* published. She meets Albert Camus at the Café de Flore. He invites Sartre and Simone de Beauvoir to contribute to the clandestine newspaper, *Combat*.
1944	Spring	'Fiestas' or writers' and artists' parties attended.

		Arrest and death of Jean-Pierre Bourla, Nathalie Sorokine's Jewish lover.
	June	Allied landing in Normandy.
	mid-July–Aug.	Sartre and Simone de Beauvoir flee Paris when the editorial secretary of *Combat* is arrested.
	11 August	They learn that the Americans are near Chartres and return to Paris to witness the Liberation.
	25 August	Allied armies enter Paris. *Pyrrhus et Cinéas* published. She becomes a founder-member of the editorial board of the new periodical, *Les Temps Modernes*, serving on it for the rest of her life.
1945	January	Sartre visits the United States: his liaison with Dolorès Vanetti ('M'). The great purge (*l'épuration*).
	19 January	She attends the trial of Robert Brasillach, executed 6 February.
	Spring	She lectures in Spain and Portugal.
	7 May	End of the war in Europe.
	August	Atom bombs on Hiroshima and Nagasaki. End of war in Far East.
	September	*Le Sang des autres* published.
	Autumn	Vogue of existentialism and Saint-Germain-des-Prés begins.
	October	French women vote in elections for the first time.
	November	Her play, *Les Bouches inutiles*, closes after fifty performances.
	Winter	She lectures in North Africa.
1946	January	General de Gaulle, head of provisional government, resigns. Her lecture tours in Switzerland, Italy, Holland — with Sartre.
	Autumn	Meets Arthur Koestler.
	November	*Tous les Hommes sont mortels* published.

1947	27 Jan.– 20 May	Her first visit to United States: lecture tour.
	21 February	Meets Nelson Algren in Chicago.
	Summer	To Sweden and Lapland with Sartre.
	15 September	Her second visit to USA: two weeks in Chicago with Nelson Algren. *Pour une Morale de l'ambiguïté* published.
1948	February	Sartre joins the Rassemblement Démocratique Révolutionnaire (RDR). *L'Existentialisme et la sagesse des nations* published.
	May–July	Her third visit to USA; she travels with Nelson Algren to Guatemala and Mexico. *L'Amérique au jour le jour* published.
	Aug.–Sept.	She travels with Sartre to Algeria.
1949	January	Kravchenko trial.
	February	Sartre and Simone de Beauvoir break with Koestler.
	June	Nelson Algren arrives in Paris; she travels to Italy and North Africa with him.
	October	Sartre quits the RDR. *Le Deuxième Sexe* published.
1950	June	North Korea invades South Korea: Korean War. Senator Joseph McCarthy's anti-Communist crusade gathers momentum in USA.
	August	Her fourth visit to the USA: she stays with Nelson Algren on Lake Michigan.
1951	October	Her fifth visit to USA to stay with Algren.
1952		Her liaison with Claude Lanzmann begins: he accompanies her on her travels.
1953	5 March	Death of Stalin.
	19 June	Execution of Julius and Ethel Rosenberg

as Soviet spies.

1954	7 May	French forces defeated at Dien Bien Phu. Opposed to French colonialism in Indochina, she is pleased.
	July	End of war in Indochina. *Les Mandarins* published.
1955		François Mauriac denounces torture practised by French army in Algeria. Simone de Beauvoir and Sartre support the Algerian Front de Libération Nationale (FLN) which engages in terrorism. Sartre is in love with Claude Lanzmann's sister, the actress Evelyne Rey.
	Sept.–Nov.	She visits China with Sartre. *Privilèges* published.
1956	February	20th Communist Party Congress in USSR: Khrushchev enumerates Stalin's crimes.
	March	Sartre meets Arlette El-Kaïm (his mistress and later his adopted daughter).
	Summer	In Rome with Sartre. Henceforward they usually spend summers in Rome together.
	26 July	President Nasser of Egypt nationalises the Suez Canal.
	5 November	Fiasco of British and French invasion of Suez. Hungarian uprising crushed by Russian tanks. She and Sartre denounce Soviet invasion of Hungary.
1957		*La Longue Marche* published.
	December	She attends trial of the Algerian Ben Saddok: considers his deed to be political assassination, not terrorism.
1958		She stands as witness for former pupil, a teacher in Algeria, accused with others of terrorist bombing.

	13 May	French army and settlers revolt in Algeria.
	30 May/ 1 June	She takes part in demonstrations against General de Gaulle.
	September	She is upset by the result of the referendum which brings General de Gaulle to power.
		Mémoires d'une jeune fille rangée published.
		Amicable separation from Claude Lanzmann.
1959	March	Protests against torture practised by French in Algeria.
1960	January	Death of Camus in a car crash.
	February	Visits Cuba with Sartre. They are welcomed by Fidel Castro.
	March	Nelson Algren visits her in Paris; stays five or six months; they visit Spain, Turkey, Greece, together.
	June	Gisèle Halimi defends Djamila Boupacha, member of FLN, who was tortured. Simone de Beauvoir takes up the case.
	August	Signs 'Manifesto of the 121' claiming the right to refuse to fight in the Algerian War.
	Autumn	Two months in Brazil with Sartre. Received by Brazilian President. Sartre proposes marriage to Brazilian girl.
	October	Second visit to Cuba.
	November	*La Force de l'âge* published.
		She meets Sylvie Le Bon (later her adopted daughter).
1961	Summer	Threats against Sartre's life.
	19 July	Plastic bomb at Sartre's flat in rue Bonaparte.
	9 September	General de Gaulle escapes assassination attempt — an undertaking which 'did not bother me much'.

1962	7 January	Second bomb at Sartre's flat; her own life is threatened.
	18 March	Evian agreement. End of war in Algeria.
	Jun.–July	Union of Soviet writers invites Sartre and Simone de Beauvoir to Moscow.
1963	January	With Sartre in USSR.
	August	With Sartre in USSR. Received by Krushchev in Georgia — he tells them off.
	October	*La Force des choses* published.
	November	She visits Czechoslovakia with Sartre. Death of her mother.
1964	Jun.–July	With Sartre in USSR.
	Autumn	*Une Mort très douce* published.
1965	February	United States at war in Vietnam.
	July	With Sartre in USSR.
1966		Sinyavsky and Daniel sentenced to Soviet labour camp.
	May	With Sartre in USSR.
	Sept.–Oct.	Visits Japan with Sartre.
	November	Attends meetings against Vietnam War. *Les Belles Images* published.
1967	Feb.–Mar.	She visits Egypt with Sartre. Received by President Nasser.
	March	She visits Israel with Sartre. Received by Prime Minister Eshkol.
	May	To Stockholm with Sartre to attend Russell Tribunal — United States action in Vietnam condemned as crime against humanity.
	June	Arab–Israeli War.
	Nov.–Dec.	Return to Russell Tribunal in Stockholm.
1968	January	*La Femme rompue* published.
	March	Visits Yugoslavia with Sartre. 'Prague Spring' — relaxation of censorship in Czechoslovakia.

	3 May	Riots at the Sorbonne.
	6 May	Student revolt — barricades.
	20 May	Invited with Sartre and others to the Sorbonne, occupied by the students.
	20 August	USSR and its allies invade Czechoslovakia.
	Nov.–Dec.	Visits Czechoslovakia with Sartre.
1969	27 April	General de Gaulle resigns.
	May	With Sartre and others she supports candidacy of Leftist student leader, Alain Krivine, for President.
1970	January	*La Vieillesse* published.
	April	With Sartre she becomes editor of *La Cause du peuple* when its editors are arrested and condemned.
	June	With Sartre she distributes *La Cause du peuple* in Paris streets.
	September	Becomes editor of *L'Idiot international* (resigns May 1971).
	Autumn	Signs 'Manifesto of the 343' — women claiming to have had an illegal abortion.
	20 November	She joins demonstration organised by Mouvement de Libération des Femmes in favour of abortion on demand.
1972	16 February	With Sartre she supports Maoist militants dismissed from Renault factory.
	June	She becomes president of 'Choisir'.
	September	*Tout compte fait* published.
1973	Autumn	Benny Lévy becomes Sartre's secretary. She begins feminist column in *Les Temps Modernes*.
1974	January	She becomes president of the Ligue du droit des femmes.
	February	Solzhenitsyn expelled from USSR.
	Nov.–Dec.	With Sartre and others she dissociates herself from Unesco because of its consistent stance against Israel.

1975	January	Awarded Jerusalem prize (for contribution to individual freedom).
	June	Interviewed by Betty Friedan.
1975–6		Various appeals made on behalf of Basque nationalists condemned for acts of terrorism, and in favour of dissident Soviet Jews who wished to emigrate to Israel.
1979		*Quand prime le spirituel* published.
1980	6 March	Marguerite Yourcenar becomes the first woman writer to be elected to the Académie Française.
	15 April	Death of Sartre.
1981		*La Cérémonie des adieux* published (together with 'Entretiens avec Jean-Paul Sartre 1974').
1983		She publishes two volumes of Sartre's correspondence: *Lettres au Castor et à quelques autres* as well as the notebook he kept during the phoney war (1939–40). She visits USA; meets Kate Millett.
1986	14 April	Death of Simone de Beauvoir.

Select Bibliography

*Works of Simone de Beauvoir**

Fiction

L'Invitée, Gallimard, 1943
Le Sang des autres, Gallimard, 1945
Tous les Hommes sont mortels, Gallimard, 1946
Les Mandarins, Gallimard, 1954
Les Belles Images, Gallimard, 1966
La Femme rompue, Gallimard, 1968
Quand prime le spirituel, Gallimard, 1979

Drama

Les Bouches inutiles, Gallimard, 1945

Non-Fiction

Pyrrhus et Cinéas, Gallimard, 1944
Pour une Morale de l'ambiguïté, Gallimard, 1947
L'Amérique au jour le jour, Morihien, 1948
L'Existentialisme et la sagesse des nations (title essay; contains also the essays 'Idéalisme et réalisme politique'; 'Littérature et métaphysique'; 'Œil pour œil'), Nagel, 1948
Le Deuxième Sexe, Gallimard, 1949
Privilèges (contains the essays 'Faut-il brûler Sade?'; 'La Pensée de droite, aujourd'hui'; 'Merleau-Ponty et le pseudo-sartrisme'), Gallimard, 1955
La Longue Marche, Gallimard, 1957
Mémoires d'une jeune fille rangée, Gallimard, 1958
La Force de l'âge, Gallimard, 1960
La Force des choses, Gallimard, 1963
Une Mort très douce, Gallimard, 1964

* Place of publication for all French titles is Paris unless otherwise stated.

133

Que peut la littérature?, Collection 'L'Inédit' 10/18, 1965 (contains her contribution to symposium)

La Vieillesse, Gallimard, 1970

Tout compte fait, Gallimard, 1972

La Cérémonie des adieux (with *Entretiens avec Jean-Paul Sartre 1974*), Gallimard, 1981

Prefaces

Halimi, Gisèle, and Simone de Beauvoir, *Djamila Boupacha*, Gallimard, 1962

Leduc, Violette, *La Bâtarde*, 1964

Steiner, Jean-François, *Treblinka*, Fayard, 1966

Juvenilia

'Un carnet retrouvé. Simone de Beauvoir élève du cours Désir', extracts discussed by Jean-Pierre Barou, *Le Monde*, 30 May 1986

Works in English Translation

The Blood of Others, Knopf, New York, 1948 (Penguin, 1964)

The Ethics of Ambiguity, Philosophical Library, New York, 1948

She Came to Stay, Secker & Warburg, London, 1949 (Penguin, Harmondsworth, 1966)

America Day by Day, Duckworth, London, 1952

The Second Sex, Knopf, New York, 1953 (Penguin, 1972)

Must We Burn Sade?, Grove Press, New York, 1953

All Men are Mortal, World Publishing Co., Cleveland & New York, 1955

The Mandarins, Collins, London, 1957 (Fontana, 1979)

The Long March, Deutsch, London, 1958

Memoirs of a Dutiful Daughter, Deutsch, London, 1959 (Penguin, 1963)

Brigitte Bardot and the Lolita Syndrome, Deutsch/Weidenfeld & Nicolson, London, 1960.

Djamila Boupacha, Macmillan, New York, 1962

The Prime of Life, Deutsch, London, 1963 (Penguin, 1965)

Force of Circumstance, Deutsch, London, 1965 (Penguin, 1968)

A Very Easy Death, Deutsch, London, 1966 (Penguin, 1969)
Les Belles Images, Collins, London, 1968 (Fontana, 1969)
The Woman Destroyed, Collins, London, 1969 (Fontana, 1971)
Old Age, Deutsch, London, 1972 (Penguin, 1978)
All Said and Done, Deutsch, London, 1974 (Penguin, 1979)
When Things of the Spirit Come First, Deutsch, London, 1982 (Fontana, 1983)
Adieux — Farewell to Sartre, Deutsch, London, 1984

Works Concerned With Simone de Beauvoir

Ascher, Carol, *Simone de Beauvoir. A Life of Freedom*, Harvester Press, Brighton, 1981

Dayan, Josée, and Malka Ribowska, *Simone de Beauvoir* (text of film), Gallimard, 1979

Evans, Mary, *Simone de Beauvoir. A Feminist Mandarin*, Tavistock, London, 1985

Francis, Claude, and Fernande Gontier, *Les Ecrits de Simone de Beauvoir*, Gallimard, 1979

——, *Simone de Beauvoir*, Perrin, 1985; (transl. edn.) Sidgwick & Jackson, London, 1987

Gagnebin, Laurent, *Simone de Beauvoir ou le refus de l'indifférence*, Fischbacher, 1968

Gennari, Geneviève, *Simone de Beauvoir*, Editions Universitaires, 1959

Hourdin, Georges, *Simone de Beauvoir et la liberté*, Cerf, 1962

Jeanson, Francis, *Simone de Beauvoir ou l'entreprise de vivre*, Seuil, 1966

Julienne-Caffié, Serge, *Simone de Beauvoir*, Gallimard, 1966

Keefe, Terry, *Simone de Beauvoir. A Study of her Writings*, Harrap, London, 1983

Madsen, Axel, *Hearts and Minds. The Common Journey of Simone de Beauvoir and Jean-Paul Sartre*, Morrow, New York, 1977

Mark, Elaine, *Simone de Beauvoir. Encounters with Death*, Rutgers University Press, New Brunswick, New Jersey, 1973

Okely, Judith, *Simone de Beauvoir*, Virago, London, 1986

Sartre, Jean-Paul, *Situations*, volume X, Gallimard, 1976

——, *Les Carnets de la drôle de guerre*, Gallimard, 1983

——, *Lettres au Castor et à quelques autres*, 2 vols, Gallimard, 1983

Schwarzer, Alice, *Simone de Beauvoir To-day: Conversations 1972–82*, translated by Marianne Howarth, Chatto & Windus/Hogarth Press, London, 1984

Whitmarsh, Anne, *Simone de Beauvoir and the Limits of Commitment*, Cambridge University Press, 1981

Zéphir, Jacques J., *Le Néo-Féminisme de Simone de Beauvoir*, Denoël/Gonthier, 1982

General Works

Aaron, Daniel, *Writers on the Left*, Harcourt, Brace, New York, 1961

Algren, Nelson, *The Devil's Stocking* (contains W. J. Weatherby, 'The Last Interview'), Arbor House, New York, 1983

Aron, Raymond, *L'Opium des intellectuels* (1955), Collection Idées, Gallimard, 1968

——, *Mémoires*, Julliard, 1983

Burnier, Michel-Antoine, *Les Existentialistes et la politique*, Collection Idées, Gallimard, 1966

Caute, David, *Communism and the French Intellectuals 1914–60*, Macmillan, New York, 1964

——, *The Fellow-Travellers*, Wiedenfeld & Nicolson, London, 1973

Cobb, Richard, *French and Germans, Germans and French*, University Press of New England, 1983

Cohen-Solal, Annie, *Sartre*, Gallimard, 1985

Contat, Michel, and Michel Rybalka, *Les Ecrits de Sartre*, Gallimard, 1970

Donohue, H.E.F., *Conversations with Nelson Algren*, Hills and Wang, New York, 1963

Friedan, Betty, *The Feminine Mystique*, Dell, New York, 1970

——, *It Changed My Life. Writings on the Women's Movement*, Gollancz, London, 1977

Goodman, Celia (ed.), *Living with Koestler. Mamaine Koestler's Letters 1945–51*, Weidenfeld & Nicolson, London, 1985

Hamilton, Iain, *Koestler*, Secker & Warburg, London, 1982

Hayman, Ronald, *Writing Against. A Biography of Sartre*, Weidenfeld & Nicolson, London, 1986

Hollander, Paul, *Political Pilgrims 1928–78*, Oxford University Press, 1981

Ivinskaya, Olga, *A Captive of Time. My Years with Pasternak*, translated by Max Hayward, Collins/Harvill, London, 1978

Koestler, Arthur and Cynthia, *Stranger on the Square*, Hutchinson, London, 1984

Lejeune, Philippe, *Le Pacte autobiographique*, Seuil, 1975

——, *Je est un autre*, Seuil, 1980

Lévy, Claude, and Paul Tillard, *La grande rafle du Vel d'Hiv (16 juillet 1942)*, Laffont, 1967

Lottman, Herbert R., *Albert Camus*, Weidenfeld & Nicolson, London, 1979

——, *The Left Bank. Writers, Artists and Politics from the Popular Front to the Cold War*, Heinemann, London, 1982

——, *The People's Anger. Justice and revenge in post-liberation France*, Hutchinson, London, 1987

McCarthy, Mary, *The Humanist in the Bathtub. Selected Essays 1937–62*, Signet, New York, 1964

Millett, Kate, *Sexual Politics*, Doubleday, New York, 1970

Pryce-Jones, David, *Paris in the Third Reich*, Collins, London, 1981

Sartre, Jean-Paul, *La Nausée*, Gallimard, 1938

——, *L'Etre et le Néant*, Gallimard, 1943

——, *L'Age de raison*, Gallimard, 1945

——, *Qu'est-ce que la littérature?* (1948), Collection Idées, Gallimard, 1966

——, *Les Mots*, Gallimard, 1963

Solzhenitsyn, Alexander, *The Oak and the Calf*, translated by Harry Willetts, Collins/Harvill, London, 1980

Todd, Olivier, *Un Fils rebelle*, Grasset, 1981

Weber, Eugen, *Action Française*, Stanford University Press, Stanford, California, 1962

Webster, Paul, and Nicholas Powell, *Saint-Germain-des-Prés. French Post-War Culture from Sartre to Bardot*, Constable, London, 1984

Winegarten, Renee, *Writers and Revolution*, Franklin Watts, New York, 1974

Index

Alain-Fournier (pseud. of Henri-
  Alban Fournier), 98
  Le Grand Meaulnes, 98
Alcott, Louisa May, 21
  Good Wives, 21
  Little Women, 21
Algren, Nelson, 67–71, 78, 110, 112,
  127,129
  The Man with the Golden Arm, 68
  The Neon Wilderness, 68
  Never Come Morning, 68
Allart, Hortense, 87
Altman, Georges, 72
Aragon, Louis, 43, 57
Arlen, Michael, 21
  The Green Hat, 21
Aron, Raymond, 25, 43, 63, 65
Audry, Colette, 45

Ballon, Renée ('Louise Perron'), 89,
  112
Balzac, Honoré de, 104
Bardot, Brigitte, 90
Barrès, Maurice, 9–10
Baudelaire, Charles, 12
Beauvoir, Françoise de (mother),
  11–17, 21, 119, 130
Beauvoir, Georges de (father), 10–11,
  13–15, 21, 42–3, 125
Beauvoir, Hélène de (sister), 11,
  14–15
Beauvoir, Simone de,
  L'Amérique au jour le jour, 67–8, 105,
  127
  Les Belles Images, 114-16, 119, 130
  Les Bouches inutiles, 63, 126
  'Brigitte Bardot and the Lolita
  Syndrome', 90
  La Cérémonie des adieux, 3, 132
  'La Condition féminine', 90
  Le Deuxième Sexe, 3, 28, 63, 82–96,
  121, 127
  *L'Existentialisme et la sagesse des
  nations*, 127
  'Faut-il brûler Sade?', 8
  La Femme rompue, 115, 119, 130
  La Force de l'âge, 3, 26, 28, 33, 42,
  46, 49–50, 52, 55–6, 58, 87, 89,
  118, 129
  La Force des choses, 3, 62, 69–74,
  78–9, 110, 118, 130
  L'Invitée, 3, 23, 29, 31, 34, 48, 50,
  54, 72, 74, 89, 98, 101–2, 106,
  118–20, 124–5
  'Littérature et Métaphysique',
  103ff.
  La Longue Marche, 75, 128
  Les Mandarins, 3, 52, 54, 60, 64–5,
  68, 70, 99, 106, 109–11, 116,
  118–21, 128
  Mémoires d'une jeune fille rangée, 3–4,
  7, 11, 17–19, 42–3, 79, 87, 102,
  29
  'Merleau-Ponty et le pseudo-
  sartrisme', 38
  Une Mort très douce, 3, 15, 130
  'Œil pour œil', 61–2, 111
  'La Pensée de droite, aujourd'hui',
  14, 105
  'Pour une Morale de l'ambiguïté',
  11, 59, 105, 127
  Privilèges, 128
  'Pyrrhus et Cinéas', 109, 126
  Quand prime le spirituel, 17, 48,
  99–100, 124, 132
  Le Sang des autres, 35, 52–3, 55, 63,
  74, 92, 106–7, 109, 116, 125–6
  'Situation de la femme
  aujourd'hui', 91
  Tous les Hommes sont mortels, 63,
  106–9, 126
  Tout compte fait, 3, 5, 35, 71,131
  La Vieillesse, 115, 119, 131
Bernard, Jacqueline, 59
Bienenfeld, Bianca, 47
Blum, Léon, 47
Bost, Jacques-Laurent, 34, 50, 124
Boupacha, Djamila, 119, 129
'Bourdin, Martine', 28, 38
Bourla, Jean-Pierre, 54–5, 126
Braque, Georges, 20
Brasillach, Robert, 51, 60–2, 126
Breton, André, 65
Brodsky, Joseph, 75
Brunschvicg, Léon, 25
Buber, Martin, 72
Buber-Neumann, Margarete, 72
Butor, Michel, 116

Camus, Albert, 57–9, 61–4, 73–4, 82,
  105, 110–11, 113, 125, 129
  L'Etranger, 57, 105
  L'Homme révolté, 73
Castro, Fidel, 76, 129